FROM THE
ATLA
COAST EXPRESS

**The insides of tunnels are difficult locations
to photograph, but the fireman on 'M7'
No 30670 obtained this view while climbing
through Black Boy Road Tunnel on 27 May
1960. Outside is Exmouth Junction yard.**
E. W. J. Crawforth

No 35010 *Blue Star* heads west from
Salisbury with the 4pm Waterloo-Plymouth
on 28 August, 1960, with the Cathedral
about a mile away behind her. The former
GWR line curves away on the left.   *K. L. Cook*

FROM THE FOOTPLATE
ATLANTIC
COAST EXPRESS

STEPHEN
AUSTIN

LONDON

IAN ALLAN LTD

Front cover:
A footplate view taken on 'Merchant Navy' class No 35027 *Port Line* at the Bluebell Railway. *Peter Zabek*

Back cover:
A classic view of the Ilfracombe and Torrington portion of the 'ACE' at Worting in 1960. *The late Derek Cross*

First published 1989

ISBN 0 7110 1822 7

Published by Ian Allan Ltd, Shepperton, Surrey; and printed by Ian Allan Printing Ltd at their works at Coombelands in Runnymede, England

Below:
Under the regulation of a fine upper quadrant signal gantry, No 34096 *Trevone* restarts the up 'Atlantic Coast Express' out of Wadebridge on Friday 8 July 1960. *J. C. Haydon*

Contents

Preface

In this attempt to revitalise a train from the skeleton of maps and timetables, I have drawn principally from the memories and records of two Southern enginemen, Mr A. E. Hooker and 'Smokey'. I hope it also benefits from association with Malcolm Collop, Melvyn Cox, the late Fred Prickett, and footplate staff, especially those of Marylebone (LMR) and Salisbury, who have shown how it is done with our preserved *Clan Line*.

I would like to acknowledge the help of British Rail (for permission to reproduce source documents), John Murray Ltd (for permission to reprint Sir John Betjeman's lines), the National Railway Museum, the Salisbury division of Wiltshire County Library, Westinghouse Signals Ltd, the Bluebell Railway, the Merchant Navy Locomotive Preservation Society, *Port Line* Locomotive Project, the Launceston Steam Railway, Mr C. J. Austin, Mr B. Beard, Mr A. C. Clare, Mr C. J. Finch, Mr

and Mrs R. Irving, Mr B. Lake, Mr S. C. Nash, Mr T. Robbins and Mr G. Ward.

The number of reference books consulted was legion and I am indebted to all their researchers, but essential reading included the *Regional History of the Railways of Great Britain Vol 1* (David St John Thomas), Oxford Publishing's *Survey of Southern Stations* (G. A. Pryer & G. J. Bowring), *Branch Line Memories Vol 1* (Lewis Reade), *Travelling on the Southern Railway* (S. N. Pike), *Bulleid Coaches in 4mm Scale* (S. W. Stevens-Stratten) and of course the columns of *Railway World* and *Railway Magazine*. Much of the source data is from the collection bequeathed by Driver Fred Prickett to the MNLPS.

Most important of all have been the support of my family, and Mr Ken Hedge on his steam typewriter.

S. H. Austin   May 1988

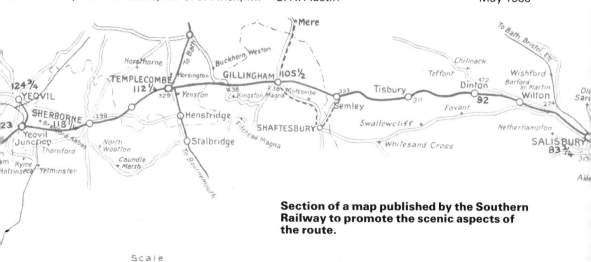

Section of a map published by the Southern Railway to promote the scenic aspects of the route.

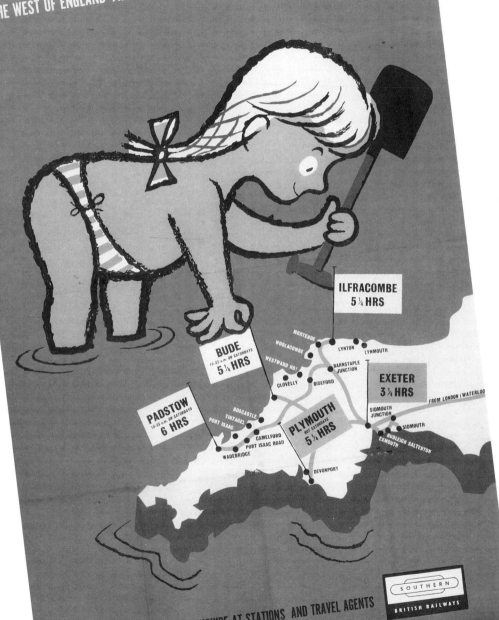

Introductory

This is a journey from London to Padstow on the 'Atlantic Coast Express'. It starts on an autumn morning in the city, whose misty dawn is tainted with the soot and sulphur of industrial and domestic hearths, for the year is 1960 and the Clean Air Act has not yet banished the memory of the London 'pea-souper'. It finishes, some 260 miles and 6½hr later, in the sea breezes of a Cornish fishing village.

For us, the day must begin long before the 11am departure of the train from Waterloo station; unlike the passengers who pay their £5 return (£7 10s first-class) to Padstow, we are going to travel in the mind's eye on the footplate of the locomotive.

We find her in London's Nine Elms locomotive depot, standing hugely immobile, emitting an occasional gurgling drip of hot water from various pipes and fittings, while from her banked-up fire a wisp of smoke rolls out of her squat chimney to mingle with smells of oil, ash, and damp wood.

At this period the West of England main line of the Southern Region (SR) is as pleasant as any for the lover of the traditional railway scene to travel over. This year of 1960 was proclaimed by Press, Radio and Television to mark a new era ('The Edge of the Sixties') and has indeed proved to be a year of change. The Prime Minister has told us that we have 'never had it so good'; we are promised a motorway network to solve all our transport problems, cheap Mediterranean holidays by jet plane, and there is even talk of landing a man on the

Below:
No 35017 *Belgian Marine* on the 'ACE' at Surbiton. The third, Ilfracombe, coach, is in carmine and cream livery; the seventh and eighth vehicles are a Tavern and Tavern Trailer. *MNLPS*

moon. In this atmosphere of progress or bust, it is little surprise that British Railways has decided that it will have no credibility unless it is seen to be getting in on the high-technology act. To admit the truth, there is little it is doing now which was not started by its predecessors before World War 2, but now it is all orchestrated under the Modernisation Plan, unveiled in 1955 and by now showing actual results. The best-publicised plank of its advance is the replacement of steam locomotives by oil engines and electric power (a process expected to take until 1980 to complete). In March 1960 British Railways proudly announced that it had stopped building steam engines, held a naming ceremony at Swindon for the last one, and never mentioned that not far away at Eastleigh, the workshops were still busy on a major refurbishment scheme for the SR's largest steam types. The latter are the 4-6-2 'Merchant Navy' and 'West Country' locomotives, examples of which in their original and modified forms will be hauling our train today. Although the SR has a few diesels and a growing electrification programme, virtually all trains west of Woking are steam-hauled. Moreover, during our journey to Padstow we see representatives of nearly all the locomotive designs which have worked the line since it became a main route to the West of England a century ago. Our passengers might reasonably expect to note about 80 steam locomotives of various sizes and ages ranging from 85 years to a few months.

We also pass through 73 stations, nearly all of which retain their original architect-designed buildings; some are impressive modern structures, but there are no specimens of the sort that appear to have been assembled by a child with a Bayko building set. And the country, apart from the London end, is as green and pleasant as you could wish and features crossings of 48 named rivers. It is a favourite journey of Sir John Betjeman, who opens his holiday reminiscences in *Summoned by Bells* by calling on us to:

Attend the long express from Waterloo
That takes us down to Cornwall. Tea-time shows
The small fields waiting, every blackthorn hedge
Straining inland before the south-west gale.
The emptying train, wind in the ventilators,
Puffs out of Egloskerry to Tresmeer
Through minty meadows, under bearded trees
And hills upon whose sides the clinging farms
Hold Bible Christians. Can it really be
This this same carriage came from Waterloo?
On Wadebridge station what a breath of sea
Scented the Camel valley! Cornish air,
Soft Cornish rains, and silence after steam . . .

Welcome to the Atlantic Coast.

This is the up 'ACE' pulling out of Salisbury. No 35025 *Brocklebank Line* is leaking steam from cylinder cocks (at the front), glands (on the side) and steam heat connection (at the rear). *B. J. Lake*

The Route

The route of the 'Atlantic Coast Express' ('ACE') had its origin in the formation of the Southampton, London and Branch Railway & Dock Company in April 1831. Its purpose, like that of the earlier Surrey Iron Railway, was to link the River Thames with the south coast for the better movement of goods, and it was one of the earliest railways to be designed for locomotive haulage. The company changed its name to the London & Southampton Railway when it opened from Nine Elms to Woking Common on 21 May 1838, and later became the London & South Western Railway (LSWR). It continued to Winchfield (24 September 1838) and Basingstoke (10 June 1839), whence it turned south for the coast; Francis Giles, the line's first engineer, was probably following the country he knew, but it must have been clear to the proprietors that it was an ideal first step towards the West Country which, at that time, I. K. Brunel and the Great Western Railway (GWR) viewed as their own property. However, the first line to reach the city of Salisbury was a branch from Bishopstoke built in 1847. This terminated in Milford on the south side, while the GWR approached the north side from Bath, and the two glowered at each other across the city while the country-side of Wessex was fought for by armies of lawyers and politicians. At one time there were four rival companies proposing schemes for a direct line to Exeter; they spent nearly £400,000 on the parliamentary battle and built not one inch of railway. It was not until the mid-1850s that the LSWR found itself the survivor in the stricken field and was empowered to proceed with the Andover to Salisbury and Yeovil to Exeter lines. The gap was filled by the Salisbury & Yeovil Railway. This company existed solely to provide a link in the Exeter route, ignoring pleas for local facilities such as a branch to Shaftesbury, and as a result it became the most prosperous railway ever. In 1878, the year it was bought by the LSWR, it paid a dividend of 14% on ordinary shares. The railway opened to Andover 3 July 1854, to Salisbury 1 May 1857, to Gillingham 1 May 1859, to Sherborne 7 May 1860, to Yeovil 1 June 1860, and to Exeter 19 July 1860. That the Exeter terminus, Queen Street, was in the city (actually in what used to be the moat of Rougemont Castle) indicates how the city's attitude to railways had changed since 1844, when it banished the Bristol & Exeter (BER) to a village down by the river called Red Cow (the Exe Valley is famous for its dairy produce).

The next section was the Exeter & Crediton Railway, a nominally independent concern known as the 'Vicar of Bray' railway because in the 30 years after its Act of Parliament of 1832 it was leased out four times, to the LSWR and B&ER alternately. Since those railways used different track gauges, the gauge was changed each time. Its eventual purchase by the LSWR was a political move to outflank the GWR empire and link up with another line which the SWR already owned. This was the Bodmin & Wadebridge Railway, one of the oldest in Britain, opened on 30 September 1834 from Wadebridge to Wenford Bridge. The LSWR adopted a policy of surreptitiously controlling this and other local companies; which included the line from Crediton to Fremington, opened on 1 August 1854, and what became the main line to Plymouth, opened to Okehampton on 3 October 1871. Railways in these parts took increasingly long times to build, owing to the rugged terrain and difficulty in raising money. The branch from Meldon to Bude was 13½ years in the making and only after it opened on 18 January 1879 was the North Cornwall Railway authorised by Parliament. The latter was extended by stages and finally brought its first train into Wadebridge on 1 June 1895, ending the isolation of the Bodmin & Wadebridge and inculcating thoughts of further expansion to the ports and resorts of Cornwall. However, that was not to be; Padstow, opened on 27 March 1899, remained the end of the line.

Such, very briefly, were the enterprises which formed the route we travel today. The system west of Exeter is known rather unfairly as the 'Withered Arm' and it is a sad fact that, after 50 years spent trying to connect the district to the rest of the country by railway, and another 50 urging people to use that railway, local railwaymen are now seeing the populace embrace their philosophy, but with cars and lorries for which they are now demanding more roads.

Below:
The fireman on No 35026 *Lamport & Holt Line* is busy as she tops the climb from Templecombe on 29 August 1964 with the down 'ACE'. The first three coaches are set No 815. As too often in later days, neither roofboards nor headboard distinguished the train. *The late Paul Riley*

The Train

The LSWR, like other railways, structured its service round an express along its main line, which started mid-morning, and which train became the company's heaviest and fastest and commanded the best in rolling stock. The first train to run from Waterloo to Exeter took 7hr, but by 1862 the best time in the timetable was 4¾hr. It went down to 4½hr in 1871, 4¼hr in 1872, 4hr in 1879, 3¾hr in 1887, 3¼hr in 1910. During the 1930s it was 3hr 2min, but World War 2 slowed things down and recovery has been very slow to the present 3hr 5min. (Next year there will be a further acceleration to 2hr 58min, and a timetable will be drawn up for 1963 showing a best time of 2hr 48min, which will never be put into effect.)

In 1925 Sir Herbert Walker, General Manager of the Southern Railway, decided on drastic action to improve the public image of the company, as the press, then as now, lost no opportunity to deride its weaknesses while ignoring its technical advances. He took the then revolutionary step of appointing a public relations officer. The man he chose, John Elliott, eventually succeeded him and probably did more for our railways than any other manager in the twentieth century. One of his campaigns was to bestow names on engines and trains. He was responsible for the 'King Arthur' names on the 'N15' class, and he arranged a staff competition to name the principal mid-morning West of England express. The title 'Atlantic Coast Express' was submitted by Guard Rowland who thus earned his niche in history; although pedants might protest that the resorts it serves are sited on the English Channel or the Bristol Channel, it is now an institution in its own right, truly an 'ACE' among trains.

For the winter 1960/61 the 'ACE' comprises nine parts on weekdays and Saturdays; with carriages to Ilfracombe, Torrington, Bude, Padstow, Plymouth, Exmouth and Sidmouth, one which is transferred to an all-stations Salisbury-Exeter train, and a kitchen and restaurant car which are removed at Exeter. On Sundays it forgets its name, stops at Surbiton, Woking, Basingstoke and Andover Junction, and runs through to Ilfracombe, Torrington and Plymouth only; passengers for Bude and Launceston have to change trains, while there are no trains at all to Padstow and Sidmouth on Sundays.

In summer the train runs in two separate parts from Waterloo: 11.0am for Ilfracombe, Torrington, Exmouth and Sidmouth and 11.5am for Bude, Padstow and Plymouth. On a summer Saturday it expands still more, with a 10.35am for Padstow and Bude, 10.45am for Seaton and Lyme Regis, 11.0am for Ilfracombe and Torrington, 11.15 for Plymouth, Padstow and Bude; but the working of this line on summer Saturdays is a subject in itself.

Although the 'ACE' is the most multiportioned train in existence, it is far from unusual in concept. In past times many through carriages linked our towns, combining with and parting from various trains in a complex interlocking jigsaw of movement, in the railways' belief that passengers disliked having to change trains. The Southern Railway developed this to an exact science, as a practical means of giving its routes a good service. There are so many lines fanning out from Waterloo that to give each one a reasonable frequency (a 20min interval service was achieved on the suburban branches) would mean cramming an impossible number of trains on to the central trunk unless they

11

Table 35   Week Days

Table 35—continued	From LONDON to THE WEST								
	pm	am	pm	am		am	am		am	am	pm
32 LONDON Waterloo dep	..		..	9 0				9 30	11 0	..
32 Surbiton	..		..	9018				9048	..	..
32 Woking				9 35				10 6		
Basingstoke dep				10 5				1045	..	
Oakley				..				1054		
Overton				..				11 0		
Whitchurch North				..				11 6		
Hurstbourne				10 28				1111		
Andover Junction				..				1121		
Grateley				..				1131		
Idmiston Halt				..				1140		
Porton				..				1142		
Salisbury { arr				10 50				1152	1223	
{ dep				10 54		11 4		Stop	1225	
Wilton South				..		1110			1120	
Dinton				..		1120				
Tisbury				..		1128				
Semley				..		1138				
Gillingham				..		1145				
Templecombe		1118		11 32		12 1				
Milborne Port Halt		1124		..		12 9				
Sherborne		1131		11 44		1217				
Yeovil Junction arr		1139		11 52		1225				
41 Yeovil Town { arr		12 6		12 6		1240				
Yeovil Junction dep				11 53		12 0				
Sutton Bingham Halt				..		12 7				
Crewkerne				..		1218				
Chard Junction arr				..		1231				
42 Chard Central { arr				..		1255				
{ dep				..		12 5				
Chard Junction dep				1222		1232				
Axminster arr				1227		1240				
43 Lyme Regis { arr				11 40		11 59				1 8
{ dep				11 40		11 40				1 55
Axminster dep				1230		1242				2 1
Seaton Junction arr				1230		1249				3 15
44 Seaton { arr				12 46		12 16				1 37
{ dep				12 31		12 50				2 2
Seaton Junction dep				1 5						2 17
Honiton				1230				1 47		2 25
Sidmouth Junction arr				1237		12 52		1 13		
45 Budleigh Salterton				1 20		1 20		2 13		
45 Exmouth arr				1 29		1 29		2 22		
45 Sidmouth dep				1 41		1 41		2 34		
				1220		12 48		1248		
Sidmouth Junction dep				1253				1 49		2 26
Whimple		1215				1 16			pm	2 32
Broad Clyst		1221				1 22		1 43		2 38
Pinhoe		1225				1 29		1 47		2 43
St. James' Park Halt		1230				1 34				25050
Exeter Central arr		1233		1 3		1 8		1 54		2 5	3 35
46 Exmouth { arr 1 11				1 42		2 11		2 41		
{ dep				12 45				1 151		45
Exeter Central dep Stop				1 14	1 26				2 10	2 20
Exeter St. David's				1 21	1 33				2 16	2 25
Newton St. Cyres				1 43						
Crediton				1 34	1 49					

Yeoford	..		..		1 58				
Bow				1 50					
North Tawton				1 57				2 55	
Sampford Courtenay				..					
Okehampton arr				2 9				3 8	
Okehampton dep				2 11				3 20	
Bridestowe				..				3 35	
Lydford				..				3 42	
Brentor				..				3 45	
Tavistock North				2 38				3 54	
Bere Alston				2 50					
Bere Ferrers				..					
Tamerton Foliot Halt				..					
St. Budeaux, Victoria Road				3 3					
Ford				..					
Devonport, King's Road arr				3 9				4 20	
Plymouth				3 15				4 25	
Copplestone				2 4					
Morchard Road				2 8					
Lapford				2 13					
Eggesford				2 20				2 50	
King's Nympton				2 26					
Portsmouth Arms				2 33					
Umberleigh				2 40					
Chapelton				2 45					
Barnstaple Junction { arr				2 52				3 16	
{ dep				2 59				3 18	
Barnstaple Town				3 4				3 23	
Wrafton				3 12				3 31	
Braunton				3 15				3 35	
Mortehoe & Woolacombe				3 33				3 53	
Ilfracombe arr				3 42				4 2	
Barnstaple Junction dep				..				3 23	
Fremington				..				3 30	
Instow				..				3 36	
Bideford arr				..				3 42	
Torrington				..				3 54	
Okehampton dep				..				3 12	
Maddaford Moor Halt				..					
Ashbury				..				3 32	
Halwill arr				..				3 39	
Halwill dep				..				3 45	
Dunsland Cross				..				3 53	
Holsworthy				..				4 2	
Whitstone & Bridgerule				..				4 11	
Bude arr pm				..				4 21	
Halwill dep 1 52				..				3 41	
Ashwater 1 59								3 50	
Tower Hill 2 6								3 57	
Launceston 2†14								4 5	
Egloskerry								4 16	
Tresmeer								4 24	
Otterham								4 34	
Camelford								4 42	
Delabole								4 48	
Port Isaac Road								4 57	
St. Kew Highway								5 1	
Wadebridge arr								5 8	
Padstow								5 21	

could be joined up into fewer, longer units as they come in and split up as they go out. Electric trains lend themselves to this treatment as they can be coupled together and driven as one or separated and driven away immediately. With steam trains there is the complication of having to attach or remove the locomotive of the rear part; at Okehampton, for example, the rear part leaves 6min after the front part, while on the up train the first part arrives at 10.57am, the second arrives at 11.13am and the whole departs at 11.19am. It seems a bit slow to the passenger who is waiting to be delivered to his destination, but he does not have to get himself and his baggage out into the weather. The through-carriage philosophy has enabled the SR to give its West Country customers a direct service to London, to counter the convenience of the private car and to keep a greater proportion of its stations open to passengers than is found elsewhere in Britain. The railwayman dislikes all this chopping and changing, of course, and would prefer to see a simple railway with fixed-formation trains shuttling independently to and fro on fixed routes. Whether the public would be prepared to patronise such a railway is open to question.

Another problem besetting all the Waterloo-West of England services is the enormous disparity between the winter and peak summer loadings. This is diminishing as foreign travel and private cars increasingly cream off the holidaymakers, but it is still of the order of four to one and looks like continuing: the only change in the 'ACE' of note in the past decade has been the closure of Plymouth Friary station in 1958, cutting the Plymouth portion back to North Road. Railwaymen at all levels believe they have a duty to cope with this imbalance. It is part of the responsibility of running a public service.

Left:
Passenger Services Timetable 1960-1961, pages 334-5 (British Railways)

The Locomotives

Our locomotive from Waterloo to Exeter is No 35028 *Clan Line*, one of the 30 'Merchant Navy' ('MN') class built under the direction of O. V. S. Bulleid, Chief Mechanical Engineer of the Southern Railway. They were intended for hauling boat trains and were named after the shipping companies which used the Railway's docks. The design required ample boiler capacity for hauling 600-ton trains, free running up to 100mph, minimum weight and kindness to the track (they were far bigger than anything run on the Southern hitherto), good conditions for the crew and reduced labour in preparation and routine servicing. The locomotives as originally constructed incorporated many unusual features, including a welded steel firebox, disc wheels, three-cylinder propulsion with chain-driven valve motion, large steam passages, multiple-jet blastpipe, a roomy cab with power-operated reverser and firedoor and electric lights. The engine was clad in a straight-sided casing which would be easy to clean from a gantry alongside, from which sandboxes and lubricators would also be filled. The first 'MNs' entered service during

Below:
The cab of *Clan Line*, seen in February 1987. Repairs were in progress, hence the firebox baffle plate up-ended on the floor and two cables entering the firehole. The steam-operated blowdown valve controls, now removed, were at the top right. *C. Austin*

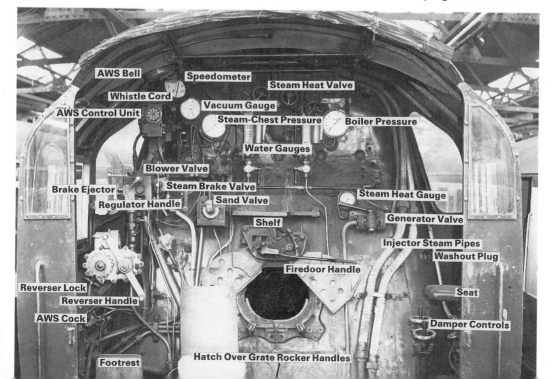

1941, working the heavy wartime freight and passenger traffic. Their performance was unprecedented, but running costs were high. They also suffered from protracted development problems which required over 150 design modifications to achieve a level of serviceability comparable with contemporary locomotives. They were therefore rebuilt, from 1956 onwards, with conventional valve motion and without the external casing.

Clan Line was built at Eastleigh in December 1948. She was based on the South Eastern routes of the SR, usually working boat trains including the 'Golden Arrow', until rebuilding in October 1959, after which she was transfered to Nine Elms. To date she has run about 450,000 miles.

From Exeter to Padstow we have No 34033 *Chard*, one of the 110 'West Country ('WC') class. They were built to the same design as the 'MNs', but some dimensions were reduced in order to lower the maximum axle weight from 21½ tons to 18¾ tons.

They are also being rebuilt, but the programme is still in progress and is destined to cease with only 60 engines treated. The rebuilds are heavier than the originals by a small margin which is sufficient to bar them from the North Devon and North Cornwall lines, so the Padstow portion of the 'ACE' requires one of the remaining originals. *Chard* was completed at Brighton in July 1946. She started work on the South Eastern and was also a 'Golden Arrow' engine until she moved westwards to Salisbury in 1948 and Exmouth Junction in 1954. Besides working westwards from Exeter she has also appeared frequently on the Brighton-Plymouth service, the longest locomotive working on the Southern. Her mileage is now around 550,000.

The 'ACE' also requires the services of other locomotives besides these two; at least a dozen will be involved in all, typically a 'Merchant Navy', two 'West Countries', two 'N' class 2-6-0s, a 'King Arthur' or 'S15' 4-6-0, two BR 2-6-2Ts and four 'M7' 0-4-4Ts, or a similar combination, varying according to the circumstances on any one day.

Below:
The BR power classification of *Clan Line* is 8P. The triangle indicates that the locomotive is fitted with water treatment.
Author

Technical Details

	'Merchant Navy'	'West Country'
Overall length	71ft 9in	67ft 4in
Total weight	151½ tons	128½ tons
Firegrate area	48.75sq ft	38.25sq ft
Boiler diameter	6ft 3½in	6ft 3½in
Boiler tube length	17ft	17ft
Heating surface area	3,116sq ft	2,667sq ft
Boiler pressure	250lb/sq in	250lb/sq in
Cylinder bore	18in	16⅜in
Piston stroke	24in	24in
Coupled wheel diameter	6ft 2in	6ft 2in
Tender coal capacity	5 tons	5 tons
Tender water capacity	6,000gal	4,500gal

The Men

Driver & Fireman

The down 'ACE' is worked from Waterloo to Salisbury by a crew from Salisbury shed No 1 Link, from Salisbury to Exeter by an Exmouth Junction Top Link crew, and from Exeter to Padstow by an Exmouth Junction North Cornwall Link crew. The top express turns are usually the preserve of the No 1 or No 2 Links. The larger depots on the Southern have six or seven links. An engineman works his way through them as a fireman and again as a driver — as long as he does not drop out on the way. The age at which he reaches the top link varies widely according to where he works: in London and the South East with cleaner and less arduous jobs beckoning, promotion is rapid and top-link firemen becoming drivers in their mid-20s are common, whereas in the rural parts they may have to wait until their late 30s to pass as driver and perhaps a year or two later to obtain regular driving duties. When a driver reaches the top link, usually in his late 50s, he can stay there until retirement, promotion to inspector or staff job (there are few such opportunities), or deterioration of health. This system puts on to the 'ACE' a fireman who is at the peak of his prowess, physically and mentally able to meet the demands of 150 tons of engine, and a driver who has experience of working all types of train under every condition likely to be encountered. Besides physical fitness, enginemen must also possess an independent spirit that relishes starting work at any hour of the day or night and working without super-vision. The only other profession that resembles it is farming, so it is no coincidence that many railwaymen are also part-time farmers — Salisbury in particular has a tradition of smallholdings. They must also be suited to bear the responsibility of the job. The aptitude for responsibility shows in another strong railway tradition, community service. Enginemen are found in town councils, churches and the governing bodies of schools, hospitals and orphanages. Not that all of them are as smart as, say, Driver Cambray of Salisbury who wore a bow tie on the footplate, or Driver Hooker of Nine Elms who changes into clean overalls before taking his engine off shed, but they are all thorough-going profes-sionals. Besides carrying a mental gazetteer of hundreds of miles of railway and thousands of signals, they have a mass of literature to understand and remember. The *Rule Book* contains 239 rules covering all aspects of the job from employment conditions, to the inspection and repair of the permanent way; from 'Absence from Duty' through to 'Yellow Lights in Signals'. The *General Appendix to Working Timetables* (a 120-page book) ranges from 'Absolute Possession of Running Lines for engineering purposes' through to 'Wrong Direction Movements in Station Limits', includ-ing the all-important 'General Regulations for Working the Standard Automatic Vacuum Brake'. The *Sectional Appendix* details special conditions and regulations applicable to parts of the system. The Working Timetables themselves include details of all scheduled movements, passenger, goods and light engines, with arrival, departure or passing times at stations and junctions. The *Weekly Traffic Notices* (details of special trains, cancellations, engineering possessions and consequent alterations) could run to a sizeable book.

When he signs on for duty a driver has another lot of information to absorb by reading the notices. Some of them are of a long-term nature, such as a prohibition on some classes of engine in certain sidings. Some are short term, such as a temporary speed restriction on a new bridge. Some are day-to-day occurrences, such as 'Whitchurch up distant signal is showing AWS fault code 2'. There may also be administrative notices such as a change in the superannuation scheme or issue of uniforms. When he has packed all this under his hat, he is ready to go out and join his engine.

Enginemen claim that one of the advantages of their job is the freedom from supervision. It is true that once they are out on the road the 'gaffer' cannot look over their shoulders, but a train in motion is not on its own; several people remote from its actual position are concerned with its progress. There is a Train Supervisor's Office at Waterloo which monitors the progress of trains by reports from signalboxes and stations where trains terminate, but it does not actively interfere with the operation of normal services unless something

Below:
The driver boards his engine. (Fred Prickett and *Clan Line*). *MNLPS*

goes wrong. There is no system of direct, centralised traffic control on the SR, a matter which has brought in a good deal of criticism in recent years. Users' groups argue that the only way to prevent localised disruptions of services is to oversee the whole railway and issue orders in the light of the overall picture. The Region's management argues that if the man on the spot had to communicate details of a situation to some distant control office and then wait for instructions back, the decision would be less precise and take longer than if he used his experience and local knowledge to sort problems out himself. It is also pointed out that no one else even attempts, let alone succeeds, in running a service as complex and intensive as the 'Southern Electric'.

As we make our way down the line, information about us is being passed along from signalbox to signalbox by means of that vital institution, the telegraph rig. A time may come when the presence of wires strung up on poles is regarded as an intolerable eyesore and the wires themselves as too vulnerable to attack by natural or human enemies. At present, however, the lineside wires are part of the scene on an active railway, as characteristic as mileposts or station gardens. The principal means of communication is the block telegraph which links block instruments in adjoining boxes and carries bell code messages. A signal out of sight of its box will have circuits for an electric repeater and a 'lamp out' warning indicator. Further wires carry current to track circuits; where the Sykes Lock-and-Block system is in use some of these run the whole length of the section. There are also several telephone lines; one between each pair of boxes, an omnibus line linking the whole route and local connections to telephones at signals, shunters' cabins, permanent way cabins or ground-frame cabins. When the 'ACE' passes, for example Overton signalbox, the signalman there transmits 'train entering section' to Whitchurch box by giving two strokes on the block bell. Whitchurch contacts the next box, Hurstbourne, and requests clearance for the train using three, pause, one on the bell for an express train. Hurstbourne acknowledges the request and sets his Whitchurch-Hurstbourne block instrument from 'Line blocked' to 'Line clear', which the instrument at Whitchurch automatically copies. Whitchurch then pulls off his down line signals. By now the train is nearing the box, and 2min later it passes. The Whitchurch signalman checks to see that it has a tail lamp and sends 'train entering section' to Hurstbourne, at the same time resetting the block instrument to 'train on line'. He resets the Overton-Whitchurch instrument from 'train on line' to 'line blocked'. Finally he sends 'train out of section' — two, pause, one — to Overton. The times of all the telegraph messages and the time the train passed his box are entered by the signalman in the Train Register book. In this way the 'ACE' is handed on from box to box through the 102 block sections between Waterloo and Padstow. The boundary between sections is not always a signalbox; on the four-track Waterloo-Basingstoke line there are remotely controlled signals at Mole bridge, controlled by Esher West; Maybury, controlled by West Byfleet and Winklebury, controlled by Basingstoke West. Also, it is perhaps a little misleading to refer to block sections in the colour-light area, for each multi-aspect signal acts as a stop signal and as distant for the signals ahead of it. Similarly, between Woking and Basingstoke the automatic signals effectively allow the eight sections to act as 20.

Within the sections are some gated level crossings whose controlling boxes are not block posts but have signals to protect the crossings, such as at Axminster Gates ('Gates' is a common term on the ex-LSWR for a level crossing). In all there are 18 controlled level crossings on the route; only one, at Wadebridge West, is on a Ministry of Transport 'A' road.

In the 48min or so it takes him to run from Waterloo to Basingstoke the driver has to observe 113 running signals. The total on the Padstow run is about 365. Many of these have subsidiary arms or lights for diverging routes, there are numerous shunting signals which do not normally apply to an express train but which may be used in the event of a breakdown or incident, and there are hundreds of other signals with which the driver will be familiar so that he can pick out the ones he needs. This adds up to a precise and rigid control of every train at all times, and its objective is — first, last and always — Safety.

Guard

Although the driver is in charge of the engine, responsibility for the train as a whole lies with the Guard. When he joins the train, he must check that the coaches are correctly marshalled and labelled, and properly coupled up. While looking at the outside, he will also check that the emergency communication gear on each coach is in the 'reset' position. He then walks through the train checking that doors are unlocked, fire extinguishers in place, etc, to his compartment, where he checks his tools: watch, whistle, notebook, carriage key, gangway key, Wrong Line Order Forms A & C, red and green flags, handlamp and detonators. Carried in the brake coach are a first aid box and heavy tool kit containing wrecking tools for use in an accident; their seals are checked. The guard then opens his daily journal with the numbers and tares of the coaches, and from then on records the running of the train, with details of any delays or untoward occurrences.

Once our train is on the move, the guard is answerable for the safety of that isolated community. All parcels and mailbags are entrusted to him and he must supervise their loading and unloading. When vehicles are attached or detached, he must see that they are fit to travel, and see that the tail lamp is in place. Train lighting and heating are under his orders; he switches the lights on and instructs the driver to supply steam heat from the locomotive. (Normally, trains are heated from 1 October to 1 May in daytime, and 1 September to 15 June at night). Before signalling the driver to start, he tests the brake using the application valve and vacuum gauge in his brake van.

The guard is as conversant as the driver is with the route, working timetables, signalling alterations, permanent way work and special traffic notices. He keeps a lookout, especially when leaving stations, and may stop the train if an emergency occurs.

In such an out-of-course stop, he has a part to play in the vital tasks of protecting the train, reporting its presence to signalmen (carrying out Rule 55), or authorising the movement of assisting engines. He is also responsible for the safety of his passengers. Any incident from a fire to somebody smoking in a non-smoking coach is dealt with by him, usually alone. Although he does not check passengers' tickets, he is supposed to assist in detection and prevention of fraudulent travel, and generally see that people and their luggage reach their destination. On multiportioned trains like the 'ACE', his duties include checking that passengers are in the right coaches, and he should call out the names of the stations — this last was a wartime measure when station nameboards were removed, and is becoming a rarity nowadays.

Once the last passengers have left the train, it is the guard who will be seen walking through the coaches shutting doors and windows and checking that everybody and their belongings are safely away. As the empty stock moves off, his day is not over, as he will supervise its journey to the carriage depot. If it is being propelled, he will ride in the end vehicle with the shunter to act as the eyes for the driver, who is then up to 260yd away behind him.

A passenger guard thus needs a wealth of experience, so he will work his way up in much the same manner as the footplate staff. Starting probably as a lad in a station or goods office, he would progress through shunter, local goods guard, express goods guard and local passenger guard to the final post in charge of top-rank expresses.

Preparation & Disposal

The SR does not, as a general rule, employ men solely for the job of making engines ready for the road and stabling them when they return, although there are a few, for example drivers who have come off the main line for medical reasons. The work is usually done by enginemen in the junior links, typically a driver not long promoted from fireman and a fireman not long promoted from cleaner. At the smaller depots, a crew may prepare an engine and work the first part of its duty, then hand over to another crew for the rest of the day and disposal. At the bigger places, a Preparation and Disposal (P&D) turn may entail preparing six or seven engines and handing them over to the main line crews ready to drive away. This is not part of some kind of footplate snobbery; it makes commercial sense to keep men who have current route knowledge out on those routes as much as possible, and it is fair to the engineman who might reasonably expect, as he gets older, to receive more of the higher-paid long distance

running and less of the dirty work. Junior crews do not spend all their time wallowing in the preparation pits, their turns also entail driving engines to and from the main station. On other days they may work shunting engines in the local yards, local goods trip working or special jobs such as ballast trains. In this way they collect a variety of experiences and a detailed working knowledge of the locomotives and the tracks on which they run. During holiday times duplicated expresses and excursions are handled by the Spare Link crews, and at busy depots such as Nine Elms, young men tackle highly responsible jobs. At such times the number of engines on the depot needing disposal or preparation may exceed the number of crews on duty to deal with them; in which case men who are on 'cover' turns (ie available on shed to take up gaps left by sickness, etc) or who have finished their turns and are interested in picking up some overtime, will be asked, persuaded or invited to pitch in and help with the P&D.

Responsibility for allocating jobs rests with the List Clerk, a sorely harrassed man who knows that whatever happens he cannot win. This man who is on a late turn wanted to change it so he could take a girl to the pictures tonight, that one wanted a night on in order to dig his allottment during the morning; one driver believes he is the victim of a plot to deprive him of his share of high-mileage work while another is always being called out on rest-days and his wife is complaining; if a job is cancelled because of lack of an engine crew there will be requests from above for explanations, but if he asks Feltham or Basingstoke to help out then the Local Departmental Committee of the union will come down on him like the proverbial ton of bricks for giving work away. Yet however close we might seem to be to chaos, the engines are always ready to work their booked trains.

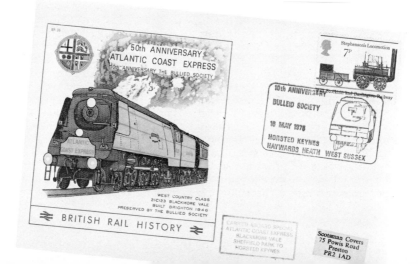

Preparation

The Train

To meet the coaches of our train, we go some four miles down from Waterloo, to Clapham Junction. From a modest beginning with the arrival of the West London Joint Railway in Battersea in 1860, this station has elevated an unpretentious London suburb to a household word, with good reason. The passenger station, with 17 platforms, covers 24¼ acres, only slightly less than Waterloo, while the total area including the yards is 35 acres, and it is by far the busiest station in the world. The number of trains scheduled to pass through in 24hr peaked before World War 2 at around 2,500 and is still always above 2,000; one every 45sec on average. Add to these empty stock trains, light engines and shunting, and it is very rare indeed for there to be nothing moving at any given moment.

Clapham carriage depot lies within the divergence of the Main and Windsor lines. It has workshops, stores and offices, with a pleasant little garden which the travelling public never sees, and 52 sidings whose four entry and exit roads pass through the station into what appears, looking eastwards from the platforms, to be a sea of metal. There are 18 parallel tracks there with a carriage washing machine standing conspicuously in their midst. The depot handles mainly main line locomotive-hauled stock. Like Nine Elms, it is fully-stretched during summer holidays and often resorts to such expedients as despatching empty trains, perhaps hauled by a goods engine borrowed from Feltham, down the Windsor line via Staines, Virginia Water, Weybridge and back up to Walton to be berthed in two long sidings on the up side

there. Now, however, dozens of surplus vehicles are being sent for overhaul, parked in the sidings or put out to hibernate in outer suburban stations; to commuters from Barnes, Richmond, et al, the appearance of a rake of carriages in their local siding is a portent of the onset of winter.

Preparation of today's 'ACE' began yesterday afternoon when the train was drawn through the carriage washer on its way into the depot. It is de rigeur for passengers to complain of dirty trains and in an era of full employment it is difficult to recruit staff for so menial a job as cleaning. There are in fact detailed procedures laid down for carriage cleaning. The outsides should be washed daily with detergent or, if very dirty, hand-washed with a chemical cleaner whose main ingredient is hydrochloric acid. The insides should be swept out daily and the trimming vacuum-cleaned fortnightly and washed every six weeks. Further instructions cover such aspects as cleaning a carriage which has been used by a passenger with an infectious disease, draining water tanks before winter storage, and so on. During the night the carriage and wagon (C&W) examiner tours the train, inspecting springs, brakes, buffers, couplings, axlebox guides, dynamo belts, vacuum hoses, bogie bolster pads, etc. He gives each wheel tyre a whack with a hammer, listening for the solid chunk of a sound one or the tinny ring of a faulty one. C&W examiners do not always work in the comfort of a shed, as they may have to seek out vehicles wherever they come to rest. Long-distance trains are sometimes cursorily examined en route with passengers aboard, and the sound of hammer on tyre has led the public to refer to the examiner as a 'wheel-tapper'.

If any carriage has a fault, or is due for routine workshop attention, the train may have to be reassembled with a replacement, then the office staff enter the details of the formation on their Daily Coaching Stock Report, which is sent to the Passenger Rolling Stock Section at Waterloo. From Waterloo, at about 9am, come the seat reservation tickets to be fitted in the train.

It is now approaching 10am, and the empty stock pilot comes on to the train: 'M7' class 0-4-4T No 30051. This engine, built at Nine Elms in 1905, is of a type designed to haul express trains between Exeter and Plymouth in 1897. However, several derailments of locomotives of this wheel arrangement cast serious doubt over their suitability for fast running, so within a couple of years they were transferred to the London suburban workings. When those were electrified they were put on to branch lines, shunting and empty stock haulage, where they have been ever since. They weigh 60 tons and are solidly built machines, but in this job they are not much liked by the crews; their acceleration is slow for shunting, and 12 full-sized coaches make a hefty load to haul to and from Waterloo. When she gets there, No 30051 will assist the departure of the 'ACE' by pushing it out of the platform, then pick up another empty train to work back to Clapham.

As our rake of carriages rolls past the Decca factory and Battersea Power Station with its 337ft-high chimneys, we can review the formation. It consists mostly of brake composites (BCKs), each seating 32 second-class passengers and 12 first-class. One end contains a guard's compartment and a luggage area surrounded by a wire mesh screen which is, naturally, called the 'cage'. A single lavatory is provided between the first and second class compartments. One vehicle thus contains all

the elements of a train. When it reaches its allotted branch line it can either go forward on its own or accommodate the guard of the branch train, but the concept is inefficient because the complete train is carrying eight empty guard's compartments which could be replaced by, say, up to 64 more second-class seats. The Torrington, Plymouth, Padstow, Bude, Exmouth, Sidmouth and Exeter coaches are all BCKs. The Ilfracombe portion consists of three vehicles: a BCK, a corridor brake second (BSK) seating 48 second-class with lavatory, guard and luggage, and a second open (SO) with 64 seats. The remaining two vehicles are a kitchen/buffet (RB) and a composite dining saloon (RCO) which operate as a pair between Waterloo and Exeter. These two, Nos 7892 and 7833 in the stock list, have a history of innovation and controversy which resembles that of the locomotive soon to haul them; all sprang from the lively mind of O. V. S. Bulleid. No 7892 was built in 1949 as the first of the Tavern Cars, in which the buffet section was decorated to adumbrate an 'Olde Englishe' pub interior with imitation wood beams, tiled floor and oak seats. The exterior had its carmine and cream livery marked with black to resemble brick courses below the waistline and timber framing above, complete with a pub sign; No 7892 was the White Horse. The dining car, termed the Tavern Trailer, continued the inn theme, but it was peculiar in having no windows except very small lights near the roof. This was deservedly unpopular — it was like eating in a baggage van — and was speedily replaced by conventional sidelights. No 7892 was refurbished last year in the style in which you see her now, the buffet interior being in the standard idiom with 11 seats and a bar. No 7833 seats 18 first-class diners and 36 second-class.

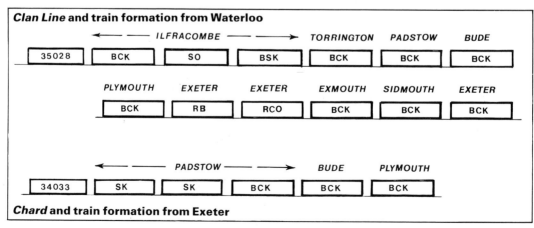

Clan Line and train formation from Waterloo

35028	BCK	SO	BSK	BCK	BCK	BCK

← ——— ILFRACOMBE ——— → TORRINGTON PADSTOW BUDE

PLYMOUTH	EXETER	EXETER	EXMOUTH	SIDMOUTH	EXETER
BCK	RB	RCO	BCK	BCK	BCK

34033	SK	SK	BCK	BCK	BCK

← ——— PADSTOW ——— → BUDE PLYMOUTH

Chard and train formation from Exeter

Bulleid main line stock

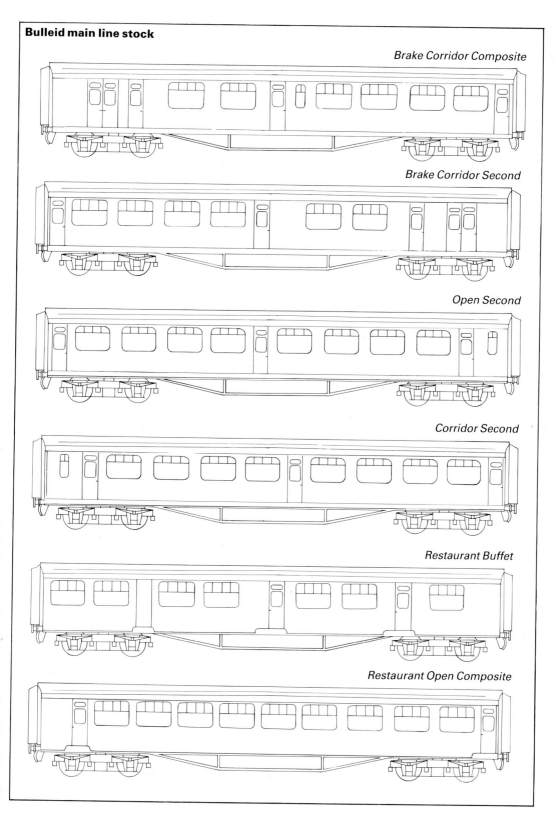

Brake Corridor Composite

Brake Corridor Second

Open Second

Corridor Second

Restaurant Buffet

Restaurant Open Composite

The train thus comprises: BCK, SO, BSK (Ilfracombe), BCK (Torrington), BCK (Padstow), BCK (Bude), BCK (Plymouth), RB, RCO, BCK (Exmouth), BCK (Sidmouth), BCK (Exeter). It seats 368 second-class passengers and 96 first-class, and weighs 408 tons. When full it will weigh in total about 445 tons, reducing to 408 tons from Salisbury to Sidmouth Junction and 370 tons from there to Exeter.

These Bulleid carriages bear some resemblance to the BR standard vehicles also seen around the Southern Region, but the likeness is superficial. Their bodies are built of wood, clad in sheet-steel sides and canvas roof, whereas the BR standard coach is an all-steel welded structure. (It is theoretically possible to dismantle a Bulleid carriage down to the underframe using only a screwdriver.) Inside, the emphasis is on brilliance, with light-toned veneers, mirrors and plenty of chromium plating, which was all very contemporary in 1945 even if it looks rather dated 15 years later.

On its way up from Clapham the train passes under three main lines and over one, all leading to Victoria. Out of sight beyond the Decca factory is Stewarts Lane, which from 1950 to 1959 was the home base of locomotive No 35028 *Clan Line*. The latter is now based at Nine Elms, the complex through which the present main line runs on a long viaduct.

The original LSWR terminus was at the north end of the site by Nine Elms Lane, and included an engine shed and goods depot, with warehouses on the riverside. When the Waterloo extension was built the station was taken for workshops and a larger engine shed. In 1861 the railway began to expand on the south side (or down) side, of the main line, where a new engine shed and workshops were built. The engine shed stood where the main line now runs. The goods depot now had the whole of the original site, but that became inadequate, so in 1877 the main line was shifted to its present position and a new engine shed was built at the south end of the works. In 1885 work began on a fifth shed, which still exists in part, in the extreme southwest corner of the railway's land and accessible only via a turntable. In 1909 all locomotive, carriage and wagon building and all overhauls were moved to a works in the country at Eastleigh, and the goods department overflowed into the workshop buildings. The present engine shed was completed with the erection of the 'New Shed' in 1910. The fifth shed, now called the 'Old Shed', was severely damaged during World War 2 and lost part of its roof. The depot as it now stands is one of the biggest in the country, with 25 roads under cover able to accommodate 95 large engines. It is equipped with the usual offices, machine shop, smithy, engine weighing table and carpentry shop. The latter has a formidable powered guillotine which chops sleepers into 12 pieces for firewood. It is here that in the watches of the night new cleaners were put through the initiation ritual of anointing with cylinder oil by their mates: here that engine No 852 was hit by a bomb and her frames bent out of shape at right angles, and was put together again: that fitters faced with a bent coupling rod on a Bulleid Pacific would put the engine by the shed wall and jack the rod an equal amount the other way so that it sprang back straight: that those most independent of men, the footplate crews, are kept in order by the personality of the Shedmaster, Mr Gilchrist, successor to the legendary J. Pelham Maitland.

Our train winds its way towards Vauxhall, the little engine working hard and the crew looking out for indicator signal WB90 on the approach to the West Crossings, hoping they will not get stopped. It is cleared into Platform 10 at Waterloo.

Many of our big stations are gloomy places, but Waterloo is bright, brash and spacious. It was not always thus. It started with three platforms in 1848 and underwent successive additions until by the 1890s there were four separate stations sprawled over 16 acres, containing 16 platforms, numerous sidings, an engine shed, four coal stages and two turntables. This was the set-up which Jerome K. Jerome satirised in *Three Men in a Boat*, with scant exaggeration although he did give it a fictitious high level. The chaos was subdued by a rebuilding, lasting from 1899 to 1922, resulting in a station completely new except for the Windsor Line section which dates from 1885. The main station at 24½ acres is the largest in Britain, with a roof 670ft by 740ft covering 21 main platforms and a vast concourse which at different times will be awash with commuters, echoing to the trundling of trolley loads of parcels and newspapers, stacked high with boxes of flowers from the Scilly Isles or regimented with holidaymakers queuing under enormous overhead letters. At no other station can you hear Winnie Atwell's piano over the loudspeakers on a Monday morning or watch the man slot in a punched card to select the display on that great Welsh dresser of a departure board. You can buy a book or a potted plant, dine elegantly in the Surrey Room Restaurant and spend an evening at the cinema, without going outside the station. And that is only part of it, for the tracks and concourse are at first-floor level.

Track diagram, Waterloo

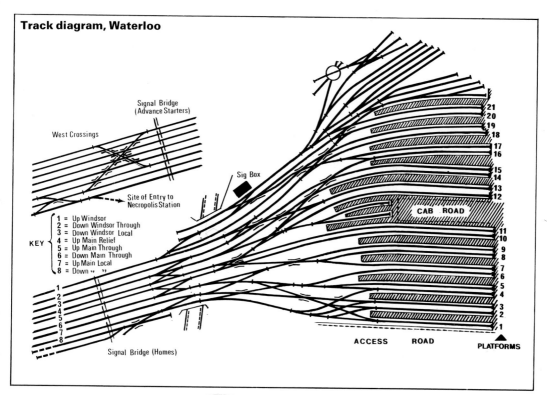

Signal Bridge
(Advance Starters)

West Crossings

Sig Box

Site of Entry to
Necropolis Station

KEY
1 = Up Windsor
2 = Down Windsor Through
3 = Down Windsor Local
4 = Up Main Relief
5 = Up Main Through
6 = Down Main Through
7 = Up Main Local
8 = Down ,, ,,

CAB ROAD

Signal Bridge (Homes)

ACCESS ROAD

PLATFORMS

Beneath is a warren of offices and stores, including a bonded liquor store. Below that is the Waterloo and City Line, and further down the Bakerloo and Northern line platforms. The South Eastern line from Charing Cross passes outside and has four platforms also called Waterloo, making a grand total of 31.

The operation of Waterloo is on a grand scale. As far as Hampton Court Junction traffic is controlled by colour-light signals with full track-circuiting and electric interlocking. The entire installation, including 390 signals, 88 route indicators, over 2,500 relays, 163 electric point machines and 518 track circuits, was designed and built by the Westinghouse Brake & Signal Co of Chippenham, and was commissioned on 18 October 1936. Three new signalboxes were built at Waterloo, Surbiton and Hampton Court Junction, 10 others modernised and their electro-pneumatic systems refurbished, and 13 boxes abolished. The showpiece is the box at Waterloo: a starkly functional building housing a 309-lever powered locking frame to control 168 points and 104 signals. (In comparison, at our destination, Padstow box has 18 levers, seven points and 10 signals.) Since it came into use there have been few changes: a locomotive yard on the down side outside Waterloo has gone, Wimbledon 'A' box was rebuilt in 1948

and when Surbiton was rebuilt in 1938 its layout was altered. There was one unique feature which has, however, vanished: the world's only railborne undertakers. The London Necropolis Co ran a huge cemetery beside the railway at Brookwood and conveyed funerals to it by special train from its own station near Waterloo. The station was situated off the Westminster Bridge Road. It and the special train were destroyed during World War 2 and the remains were removed a few years ago.

The Engine

An argument which some ignorant people raise in the 'diesel versus steam' controversy, which is in full swing among armchair enthusiasts although British Railways have long since made their decision, is that the steam engine will work with very little maintenance. It is unjust to the many skilled men who work day and night to keep our engines running. Nine Elms locomotive depot has around a hundred such: boilersmiths and their assistants, coppersmiths, carpenters, boiler washers, brickarchmen, fitters, assistant fitters and labourers. They sustain a continu-

23

ous cycle of examinations and component replacements on every engine, all the time it is in service.

Preparation of *Clan Line* for her run to Exeter really begins when she arrives on the depot after her previous turn of duty. The driver disposing her makes a systematic examination of all moving parts, looking for loose fastenings, missing split pins, signs of lack of lubrication, blowing pipe joints, etc. If there are any 'knocks' in the motion he will check where they are; if there is anything wrong in the exhaust beat of the engine he will, by setting her in an appropriate position and opening the regulator slightly with the cylinder cocks open and handbrake hard on, check for damaged piston or valve rings. The fireman who removes the fire looks for damage to the brick arch or leaking boiler stays, and when he empties the smokebox he looks for any sign that pipe joints have been blowing, boiler tubes leaking or smokebox door admitting air. Any defects they find, and any faults noted by drivers on the road, are entered on a report card which goes into the mechanical foreman's office. There they are divided into mechanical work, passed to the chargehand fitter, or boiler work, passed to the chargehand boilersmith. Even if there are no repairs, there is a schedule of routine inspections which ensures that every part of an engine is examined at intervals based on the miles run or time in use. The schedule is laid down in British Railways Circular MP11 *Standard Examinations of Steam Locomotives*. It lists 148 items, besides the daily examination which is basically a visual inspection of the locomotive and a check of the functioning of the controls. Examples of items examined every 6-8 working days are axlebox underkeeps, grease lubrication points (86 on a 'Merchant Navy'), rocking grate mechanism and springs; every 12-14 days boiler water gauge glasses are changed; every 3-5 weeks a thorough inspection of the brake system; injectors are stripped and tender tanks cleaned out every 7-9 weeks; connecting and coupling rods are examined in position every 20-24,000 miles, and every 40-44,000 miles they are taken down, bushes checked for wear, pistons and valves checked and rings renewed. The boiler, with a working pressure of 250lb/sq in, contains a power that must be treated with utmost respect. At the weekly examination a boilersmith gets into the hot firebox and smokebox to tap the stays and tubes and inspect the seams. Every 56 days the boiler is emptied and 28 screwed plugs and four mudhole covers are removed so that it can be washed out with a high-pressure water

supply and inspected internally for sludge or scale. A chart is kept showing the history of every stay, tube and rivet, and if at any time the boilersmith entertains any doubt about the integrity of any part of the boiler, the engine is 'stopped', without argument. In any case, no boiler spends more than three years or so in service before it is lifted out of the engine for replacement of some or all tubes and stays. Only if all the examinations have been signed up to date on the engine record cards will *Clan Line* be placed on No 6 duty — the down 'ACE' — for the following day.

At about 8.50am a driver and fireman of No 5 Link arrive to prepare *Clan Line*. She is standing in the roofless area of the 'old' shed, where the shed turner left her, with a small banked-up fire, pressure about 100lb and water level at about three-quarters the height of the gauge-glass.

They bring into the cab two oil bottles, a bundle of cotton waste, a flare lamp and a firing shovel. The first thing they do is to ensure she is secure with the handbrake on, and the fireman checks the boiler water level. It is vital that the firebox be kept covered with water while there is a fire in it. The gauge-glasses are positioned so that when the water level reaches their bottom nuts the firebox crown has about 6in of water over it, and it is the fireman's first and constant duty to keep the water in sight in the glass. The better to see it he opens the steam valve to the electric lighting generator, which starts up with a rumble like a departing Underground train and settles to a steady whine. He places an oil feeder of engine oil and a clean cloth on the firedoor tray and uses the flare lamp to look inside the dark firehole. He checks that the grate is free from clinker and that there is no sound of steam leakage from tubes or fusible plugs, and then he extracts a long rake from its stowage in the tender, runs it over the firebars to clear any cinders and begins to spread out the smouldering fire. Taking a hand brush and a heavy bar he leaves the footplate, uses the bar to operate the hopper ashpan to see that it is empty, then climbs up on to the tender to check that it has been filled with coal and water and see whether there are any decent lumps in the coal. The brush is to clear any stray coal from the cab roof or tender top. Now back to the cab and use the coal-pick to knock out three catches closing a door in the tender front, whereon coal cascades into the cab. He starts to feed the fire, pushing the burning mass over as it catches, opens the rear ashpan damper and eases the blower handle over. Up at the front end a shower of sooty water from *Clan*

Line's chimney is followed by a soft deep hissing and an energetic billow of smoke. The fireman comes to check that the smokebox door is tight and the front platform swept clear. After making up the fire some more, he checks the tools; bucket, brush, spanners, fire-irons, clinker shovel, oil lamps, paraffin bottle, red flags, detonators, etc. The chances are that something will be missing, so he goes off to the depot stores and also visits the sand drying plant for a bucket of sand. A 'Merchant Navy' carries 3½cwt of sand, sufficient to flow for about 15min.

The driver carries out the oiling and examination of the engine. There are 69 oiling points, including seven on the inside valve motion between the frames. To reach those is

Above:
Underneath a 'Merchant Navy', looking forwards to the middle coupled axle springs. The axle is out of sight behind a frame cross-member. Every item in this view, and many more, must be regularly inspected. Photographed on *Clan Line* in 1973. *Author*

Right:
Filling the right-hand leading sandbox.
C. Austin

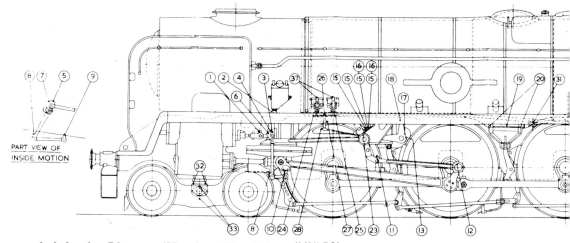

Lubrication Diagram, 'Merchant Navy' class (MNLPS)

PART VIEW OF INSIDE MOTION

IDENTITY NUMBER	DESCRIPTION	POSITION OF NIPPLES	No. OF POINTS L.H	MIDDLE	R.H
1	PISTON VALVE CROSSHEAD PIN	ON CONNECTING LINK (FRONT)	1	–	1
2	SUSPENSION LINK PIN	ON SUSPENSION LINK	2	–	2
3	CONNECTING LINK TO SUSPENSION LINK	ON CONNECTING LINK (REAR)	1	–	1
4	COMBINATION LEVER TO SUSPENSION LINK	ON COMBINATION LEVER (TOP)	1	–	1
5	COMBINATION LEVER TO RADIUS ROD	ON COMBINATION LEVER (TOP)	–	1	–
6	COMBINATION LEVER TO RADIUS ROD	ON COMBINATION LEVER (TOP)	–	1	–
7	COMBINATION LEVER TO P.V. CROSSHEAD	ON COMBINATION LEVER (TOP)	–	1	–
8	COMBINATION LEVER TO UNION LINK	ON COMBINATION LEVER (BOTTOM)	1	1	1
9	UNION LINK TO CROSSHEAD ARM	ON UNION LINK (REAR)	1	–	1
10	CROSSHEAD ARM TO UNION LINK	ON CROSSHEAD ARM	1	–	1
11	ECC ROD TO PIN (OUTS) ECC ROD TO TRUNNION (IN)	ON ECCENTRIC ROD		1	
12	RETURN CRANK ROLLER BEARING	ON BEARING COVER PLATE	1	–	1
13	REVERSING SHAFT	SHAFT BEARINGS ON OUTS. MOTION BRACKET	2	–	2
14	REVERSING HANDLE SPINDLE	ON REVERSING HANDLE SPINDLE	1		
15	EXPANSION LINK BEARING (LH & MIDDLE)	ON MOTION BRACKET	4	–	–
16	EXPANSION LINK BEARINGS R H	ON MOTION BRACKET	–	–	2
17	REVERSING SHAFT SPRING BALANCE PIN	ON SPRING BALANCE ARM	–	1	–
18	REVERSING ROD FRONT PIN	ON END OF PIN	1	–	1
19	REVERSING SCREW NUT	ON REVERSING SCREW NUT	1	–	
20	REVERSING SCREW BEARINGS	ON REVERSING SCREW BRACKET	2	–	

IDENTITY NUMBER	DESCRIPTION	POSITION OF NIPPLES	No. OF POINTS L.H	MIDDLE	R.H
21	ROCKING GRATE OPERATING LEVER PIN	ON OPERATING LEVER	1	–	1
22	DAMPER OPERATING SCREW & TRUNNIONS	ON DAMPER CONTROL COLUMN			4
23	LUBRICATOR DRIVING ARM PIN	ON LUBRICATOR DRIVING ARM	1	–	1
24	RATCHET ARM. TO DRIVE PIN (FRONT)	ON RATCHET ARM	1	–	1
25	RATCHET ARM. TO DRIVE PIN (REAR)	ON RATCHET ARM	1	–	1
26	LINK PIN	ON LINK	1	–	1
27	BRACKET TO INTERMEDIATE DRIVING SHAFT	ON BRACKET	2	–	2
28	INTERMEDIATE LEVER TO INTERMEDIATE PIN	ON INTERMEDIATE LEVER	1	–	1
29	COUPLING TRUNNIONS (REAR)	ON COUPLING	1	–	–
30	COUPLING TO SPLINE SHAFT	ON COUPLING	1	–	–
31	COUPLING TRUNNION (FRONT)	ON COUPLING	1	–	–
32	BOGIE SLIDING CENTRE	ON SLIDING CENTRE	–	4	–
33	BOGIE SIDE CONTROL GEAR	ON END COVERS AND STRETCHER	1	2	1
34	TRAILING TRUCK RADIAL PIN	ON TRUCK & ENGINE FRAMES	–	2	–
35	TRAILING TRUCK SIDE CONTROL GEAR	ON END COVERS & TRUCK FRAME	1	4	1
36	INTERMEDIATE BUFFER (ENGINE)	ON CAB UNDERFRAME (LH SIDE)	2	–	–
37	MECHANICAL LUBRICATOR DRIVE RATCHET	ON TOP OF OUTER GEAR CASE	2	–	2

a filthy job for which some drivers keep a second set of overalls. If the engine is moveable, the easiest access is obtained by positioning her at just above back dead centre on the right side and winding the reverser to 55% back gear. One or two oil-box corks need replacements which he is carrying in his pocket, and if any worsted trimmings are dirty or damaged he will fit new ones. As he works his way round the engine he is looking out for faults. He leaves nothing to luck or to assume someone else has checked it; the safety of a trainload of people is his responsibility. He is also keeping an eye on the comings and goings of his fireman, for whose work he is responsible. A visit to the cab to replenish his oil feeder gives an opportunity for some coaching with his young mate in the art of flicking coal into the back corners of the firebox — 'Do you hear it hit the side?' One of the two oil bottles contains cylinder oil, a substance like dark green treacle so thick that it is stood on the shelf over the firehole for half an hour to warm before pouring it into the Wakefield mechanical lubrication pumps on the engine gangway. While he is up there the driver pauses to admire the 6ft-long nameplates with their beautiful enamelled flags. There is very little cleaning of engines, of the old style, at

Above:
Driver Fred Prickett, then retired, oiling round *Clan Line* during a post-preservation steaming. *A. Davies*

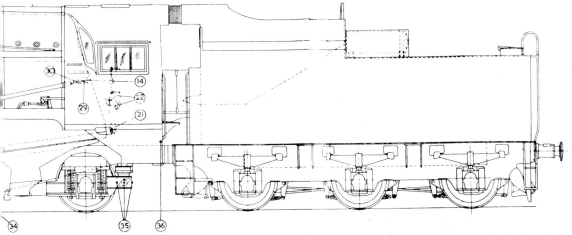

Nine Elms these days, although as this is a prestigious duty a cleaner is assigned to give her a general once-over with paraffin followed by oil-soaked cloths, and she looks fairly smart. He is at work when the preparation crew arrive, so they send him on a few errands including fetching an 'ACE' headboard and a couple of clean headcode discs. Cleaning up the footplate is traditionally a job for the fireman. When he has packed his coal avalanche into the firebox and got the tender door shut he sweeps up the dust, washes the floor, rubs over all the gauges and handles and filches a spot of cylinder oil to put a shine on the boiler backhead. He shuts off the boiler water gauges and removes and polishes the plate-glass protectors. The glass tubes of the gauges, connected directly to the boiler, are the most vulnerable items on the engine, hence the triple precaution of ball-valves which should close if a glass bursts, manual cocks and outer protectors. Lastly, even if he has time for nothing else, he will make sure the right hand tender cupboard is clean, because that is where the main line crew put their bags and coats.

For a while, the boiler pressure does not respond to the fireman's ministrations, indeed it may fall slightly owing to steam consumption by the blower, but when the fire gets going and produces flames instead of smoke, it rises fast. It is now time to test the auxiliaries. The morning air is split by the roar of a Davies and Metcalfe No 11 'Monitor' injector, then there is a metallic bang as it is shut off, followed by a similar performance from its companion. If either injector does not start cleanly the driver will not take the engine off the shed. He opens the vacuum ejector steam valve (another Davies & Metcalfe product, a Type RM combination ejector and graduable steam brake

Above:
Mechanical lubricators. The lid of the Wakefield No 7 lubricator is open, beside it is an oil bottle with a length of worsted tied to its handle to show that it contains cylinder oil. *C. Austin*

Below:
The right-hand side showing injectors with their delivery pipes, rear truck and ashpan with damper operating rods. Between engine and tender are a main drawbar, two safety links, two water pipes, two vacuum pipes, steam heat pipe and an electric cable. *A. Davies*

Left:
**Injector controls, fireman's side. The shafts
go through the floor and the left-hand one,
for steam control, has been removed. The
small handle works the coal spray; further
left is the steam control for the other
injector, also minus its shaft.** *C. Austin*

Below left:
**Steam sand control, with blower handle
above and to the right.** *C. Austin*

valve) and is startled by a loud squawk above
his head. The Automatic Warning System
(AWS) has only been in general use on the SR
for a short time — it was fitted to *Clan Line*
some six months ago. A detailed description of
this gadget would be out of place here, but
essentially it relays signal aspects to the
engine cab. Electromagnets on the track
activate a magnetic switch on the engine; a
'clear' signal rings an electric bell in the cab for
2sec, a 'caution' signal operates a solenoid
which admits air through a siren to a vacuum
reservoir and, if the driver does not operate a
reset switch, applies the vacuum brake and
stops the train. The equipment on the engine is
powered by an alkaline battery which is
changed every five weeks. It is the only system
whose working the driver is not expected to
understand in detail; it either works or does
not, and if it does not he cannot create vacuum
at all. Today all is well, he pulls the reset
handle and the vacuum gauge needles rise to
indicate 21in of vacuum in both train pipe and
main reservoir. The basic brake test comprises
shutting off the ejector to see that the train pipe
is not leaking, then applying the brake to prove
that the tender vacuum brake cylinders operate
without leaking air to the reservoir, and that
the engine steam brake comes on at the same
time.

Before the engine is moved off the preparation pit there is another job to do; blowing
down the boiler. To prevent formation of scale
in the boiler, chemicals are added to the water
to precipitate impurities, mostly calcium com-
pounds, in the form of a soft sludge which is
easily flushed out from the lowest point in the
boiler, the firebox front. The treatment chemical is in the form of briquettes carried in a
perforated can inside the tender which allows a
controlled release into the water. The process
is managed by the Water Treatment Controller
who takes water samples from engine boilers
and the depot supplies, issues briquettes and
adjusts the tender units. With over 100 engines
to look after, he gets plenty of overtime.

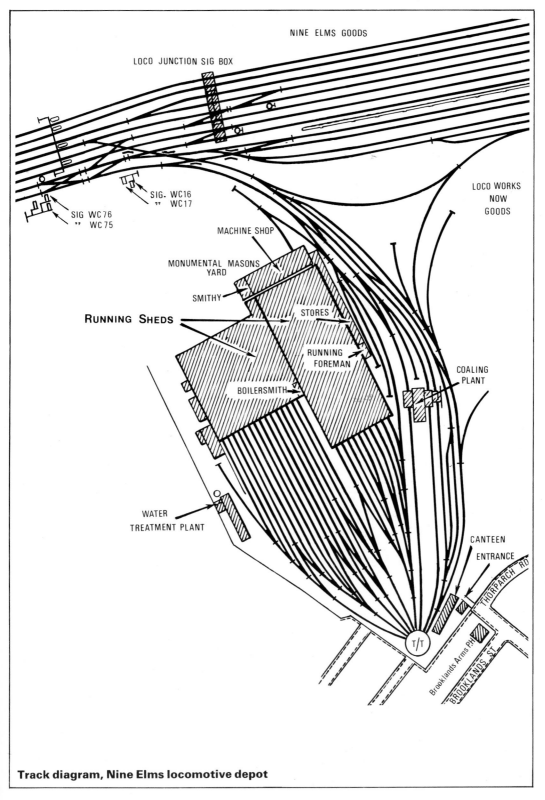

Track diagram, Nine Elms locomotive depot

Right:
These notices are fixed in the cab roof on the driver's side, by the cab light switches. They are preserved on *Clan Line* in 1987. *C. Austin*

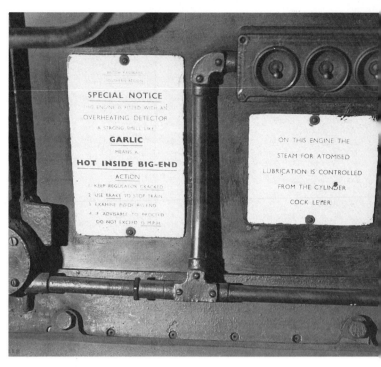

SPECIAL NOTICE

THE ENGINE IS FITTED WITH AN
OVERHEATING DETECTOR
A STRONG SMELL LIKE
GARLIC
MEANS A
HOT INSIDE BIG-END
ACTION
1 KEEP REGULATOR CRACKED
2 USE BRAKE TO STOP TRAIN
3 EXAMINE INSIDE BIG-END
4 IF ADVISABLE TO PROCEED
DO NOT EXCEED 15 M.P.H.

ON THIS ENGINE THE
STEAM FOR ATOMISED
LUBRICATION IS CONTROLLED
FROM THE CYLINDER
COCK LEVER

A 'Merchant Navy' has two blowdown valves, a power-operated one which we shall see in use later and a manual one which the fireman operates from the ground. Before doing so he double checks that no one is in the pit nearby, and the engine whistle is blown as a warning, because the process is potentially very hazardous. Water in the boiler is at a temperature of 200°C, so as it is released to atmospheric pressure it flashes instantly into steam. The ground shivers and for 20sec the engine disappears in a white cloud with a roar that echoes round the shed. As it subsides he walks over to the turntable to hand-crank it round into alignment with our track, then trudges back to the cab where the back injector is singing and the driver is drawing a bucket of hot water to wash his hands. He climbs up the tender ladder to drop the pipe of the nearby water column in the tank. Blowing-down and refilling the boiler has taken about 400gal of water. Replenishing the tank only takes a few seconds, and now we are ready to go. The fireman tries to unscrew the tender handbrake, which he cannot do because it was screwed down while the vacuum brake was on, so the driver 'drops the handle' to free the linkage so he can release it. The driver winds the reversing handle into back gear and, with both men keeping a good lookout, tugs the regulator handle open until *Clan Line* gives a very human sigh and steam begins to jet from

the cylinder drain pipes. The noise is considerable, but that has nothing to do with the movement of the engine; a steam engine, unlike other currently fashionable prime movers, develops its power in silence. When she is ready, *Clan Line* moves off slowly backwards.

With one hand on the regulator and one on the brake he eases very gently on to the turntable to stop in the right place, give or take a few inches. The fireman climbs down and quickly connects one of the engine's vacuum hoses to the vacuum-powered turntable machine, shouts 'Blow up, mate', and works the controls as *Clan Line* uses the power of her brake ejector to rotate herself. Since she is facing north she has only to be turned about 60° before moving off. This having to use the turntable to enter or leave the old shed is a major inconvenience; it is possible to get out from the far side of the shed without using it but that entails 11 reversals. The table is right in a corner of the site and if you run over it you will find yourself out in Brooklands Road.

By now a good ton and a half of coal has gone into the firebox, so the next stop is under the coaling plant to top up the tender. This steel and concrete structure is a prominent feature in pre-highrise London. It incorporates a hoist which lifts a coal wagon and tips it bodily over a hopper with a capacity of 400 tons. Repairing the machinery at the top is one

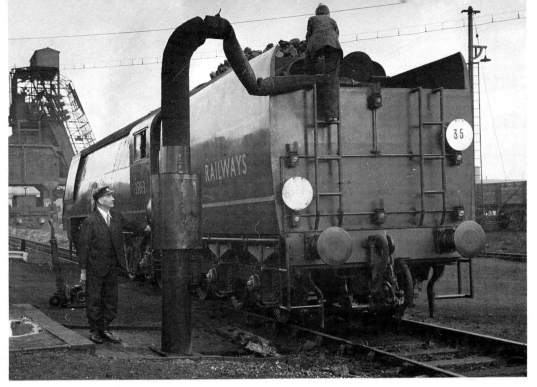

Above:
Watering No 35013 *Blue Funnel* at Nine Elms on 20 September 1948. Headcode discs are already in place on the tender.
British Railways

Below:
At Nine Elms, No 34063 *229 Squadron* eases on to the turntable. She has arrived from Waterloo and is carrying a tail lamp on the front. In the left background are the New Shed and the coaling tower. The big cylinder strapped to the turntable is a vacuum reservoir. *MNLPS, Prickett Collection*

of the jobs which are often given to the boilersmiths because they are qualified welders, but it is not popular; the view is superb but at least one man has fallen to his death from the top. Beneath it the track foundations are so thoroughly imbued with coal dust that drainage is non-existent (actually the whole site suffers from chronically poor drainage) and the track is subsided and uneven. The majestic sight of a locomotive leaving the depot is often reduced to an undignified slither to a complete standstill while trying to climb out from the coal road. In wet weather it is advisable to back out to the ashpit and then take a run at the slope.

If all goes well, preparation should be completed by about 10.15am, giving the fireman time to make some tea before departure at 10.25am. The fire is built up well to the back, the damper partly open and the firedoors ajar to prevent smoke, boiler pressure is 180lb and rising slowly. Building the fire so that it is the right depth, burnt through and a full head of steam at train time without unnecessary blowing-off beforehand, is a matter of judgement based on experience of the type of engine and the variety of coal in use.

'At that time Nine Elms was using either Bedwas or second-grade Welsh. It wasn't too bad.' — A. E. Hooker.

The Loco Junction signalman has pulled off the shed exit signals and is looking out for *Clan Line*. At 10.25am she comes up into the 'Waterloo siding' with a tail lamp on the front and headcode discs on 1 and 5 positions (top and centre bottom) on the back of the tender, denoting a light engine heading for Waterloo for a West of England train. The signalman has to reset nine point levers to give us the road on

to the up main through, then signal No 76 clears, and with a blast on the mellow Bulleid whistle the 'ACE' engine moves off. (As she sets out from the depot, about 22½% of her total weight, some 34 tons, consists of water.)

Clan Line swings out on to the up main through line, her fully laden tender jerking uneasily over the crossovers under Loco Junction signalbox. Speed for the run up to Waterloo is around 30mph with the regulator just open and reverser set to 30% cut-off to avoid producing a strong exhaust blast which would fan the fire into life before it was wanted. Both men ride standing on the pivoted plate which bridges the gap between engine and tender, so that they can get the best view through small windows in the tender front which give some rear view without leaning out. To a footplate passenger accustomed to riding in motor cars, the sight of an engine going along quite happily with no one holding any of the controls is at first somewhat unnerving.

The Loco Junction signalman telephones to Waterloo box: 'Light engine for the eleven o'clock'. The Waterloo supervisor takes the call and says 'Up Main Through to come in Number Ten'. One of the three signalmen, who is keeping an eye on the engine's approach on his track diagram, waits until the track-circuit indicator lights show that she is approaching

Below:
Waterloo signalbox interior when it was new in 1936. Four signalmen are at the levers, two juniors keeping train registers at the small tables, and a supervisor on the left.
Courtesy Westinghouse Signals Ltd

A contrast with the Bulleid cab is provided by this view of the preserved 'T9' No 30120. Scant protection from the weather, regulator handle in the centre of the backhead and a hydrostatic lubricator on the right are points of interest. The fireman is working with the Drummond firedoor, which hinges upwards. Photographed on the Mid-Hants Railway in April 1988. *P. Zabek*

Left and below left:
**Hitching up and tightening a screw
coupling: a scene posed on the Bluebell
Railway.** *C. Austin*

and superheater to move the engine while he controls her with the brake. Backing on very slowly with steam on in this manner avoids the possibility of the engine being bounced back by the buffer springs, with consequent waste of time easing up again. In the 'MN' the volume of superheater header, elements, connecting pipes and steam chests is large, engendering a long delay in response to the regulator. Added to the response time between moving the brake handle and the blocks gripping the wheels, this means that to move the engine an inch or two entails opening and shutting the regulator and then dropping the brake handle before she actually starts to move; it is not very easy.

The fireman waits on the ground until the engine is firmly in position and a blast of steam exhausting beside the ashpan indicates that the driver has opened the cylinder drain cocks. He raises a hand and gets an answering wave from the cab window — a seemingly casual but vital safety procedure before he goes between the vehicles to couple up. The first action in coupling is to lift both engine and carriage vacuum hoses off their dummy couplings, thus immobilising both. He lifts the screw coupling, permanently attached to the tender drawhook, across to the carriage drawhook, taking care to keep his fingers clear of the hook and of the coupling pivots, and screws it up till it is just horizontal and will keep the buffer heads together. He grasps one vacuum hose in each hand and brings them up at an angle so that their couplings interlock, with the ears crossed and the slotted prongs dropping past each other. A spring clip is pushed into each slot. The steam heat hoses he leaves unconnected because we are not yet into what is officially described as the carriage-warming season. The coach also has a buckeye type coupler which is not used but left hanging down in its stowed position.

Incidentally, it is also necessary for the empty stock pilot engine to be uncoupled from the other end of the train. No published report has been found of a pilot driver reaching the platform end and discovering he has forgotten this detail, but it must have happened at some time. The writer has seen the converse occur at Paddington, when an engine made a vigorous start, an abrupt stop and an insouciant return to collect its train, but the Great Western always did have a special way of doing things.

the inner home signal before he pulls lever No 85. The disc subsidiary signal comes off and an indicator panel beside it lights up with a '10'. A check out of the window shows the engine moving slowly towards the end of her train. The compromise forced on the designers of Waterloo by the cramped nature of the site — in spite of their demolishing a couple of streets of houses and a church — is evident in that the first coach is partly off the end of the platform; the engine will be beyond the starting signal so a platform supervisor will have to relay the signal to the driver. A train longer than 13 coaches extends into the next track circuit section, preventing the signal from being pulled off, and has to be signalled away by hand.

Clan Line comes almost to a stop about 6ft away from the coach end and the fireman climbs off while the driver, watching out of his small side window with one hand on the brake handle, brings her back just hard enough to compress the buffers slightly but not to move the coach. He has the regulator shut and is allowing steam pressure in the steam chests

Our fireman completes his business by taking the two headcode discs round to the front and placing them on top and bottom middle brackets — the headcode for Waterloo to Exeter and Plymouth — and removing the tail lamp. Meanwhile, at the business end, the station announcer is reciting an Arthurian liturgy of names: '. . . Egloskerry, Tresmeer, Otterham, Camelford. . .' A station inspector arrives to advise the guard that he has a disabled lady passenger to Launceston. She explains that she prefers to travel by the SR route because it does not subject her to a change of train, which is quite true, but it is also true that had she gone on the 10.30am 'Cornish Riviera Express' from the Other Place, she would not reach Launceston until 4.39pm, a journey over an hour longer. There are no special facilities for the disabled on British Railways trains at this time, nor is information published on which stations are convenient for them. She has to be helped to her seat by one of the volunteers from the station ambulance room, since the doors and corridor will not admit a wheelchair although it travels free in the baggage area if it is of the folding type.

The guard proceeds down the platform, pausing to advise three parties that they are in the right coach and 17 that they are in the wrong one, to cast a critical eye over the coupling between engine and train and to meet the Salisbury driver and fireman, who worked up earlier this morning. He takes the driver's name for his journal and states that the load is '12 440 tons', and turns away with a request: 'Give us a brake, would you?'

The Salisbury fireman climbs aboard *Clan Line* and is greeted by the Nine Elms men. He looks in the firebox and slams the door shut, to the evident relief of the preparation fireman. The driver enters, stows his bag in a tender cupboard, turns on the vacuum ejector small jet, wipes the driving seat with a clean cloth and sits making notes on his ticket while watching the vacuum gauge. It takes some time to evacuate the whole train pipe and 26 brake cylinders, but although the vacuum ejector has a second jet for faster release there is no point in using it because if the small jet cannot create vacuum now it will not be able to sustain it while running. The needle reaches 21: at this stage it would be surprising if it did not. A couple of minutes later it sags and then recovers as the guard tests his brake application valve. The driver tries the brake from this end, then steps down for a look round the engine.

One point before we start — this train journey is not a race, either against the clock or against other people. The schedule is laid down so it can be followed not just today but every day, in all weathers, by engines split-new or coming up to overhaul, using coal from the best layer of a seam or the worst, handled by men who may be feeling at the top of their form or may not. Crews expect to run on time; they generally try to recover delays, but thrashing engines along in disregard of the timetable is not accepted practice. The schedule follows on page 38.

Below:
On 13 March 1964, *Clan Line* stands at Waterloo's Platform 9 ready to depart. On this day she was commendably clean, although the headcode discs leave a little to be desired. Inspection shows the headboard to be slightly battered along the top edge, where a few smart taps would be customary to sit it down on the brackets. A. Muckley

Above:
The South Western look is re-created by the Mid-Hants Railway in 1986; 'Greyhound' No 30120 and BR Standard Mk 1 coaches in late 1950s colour scheme pass a LSWR lattice-post distant signal. The headcode discs proclaim Padstow, although the location is actually Ropley. *P. Zabek*

Right:
The author on *Clan Line* at Hereford, 9 December 1984. *E. W. J. Crawforth*

Below right:
The down 'ACE' passing Sutton Bingham reservoir on 13 June 1964. The engine, No 35017 *Belgian Marine*, has, typically, had the cabside numbers cleaned. *H. Ballantyne*

Above:
'West Country' No 34032 Camelford climbing Honiton Bank with the 12-coach 11.45am Waterloo-Ilfracombe on 27 June 1964. A 'West Country' would have to be pushed a little harder than a 'Merchant Navy', but would still be master of the job.
H. Ballantyne

Below:
At the east end of Salisbury station, No 35003 Royal Mail is seen getting away with the Sunday 10.10am Plymouth-Waterloo, and slipping in spite of having the steam sanders on. Photographed on 8 March 1964. *H. Ballantyne*

'ACE' Schedule Timings

Miles				Required average speed (mph)
0.0	Waterloo	dep 11.0am		
				33 start-pass
3.9	Clapham Jn	pass 11.7am		
				52 pass-pass
13.4	Hampton Court Jn	pass 11.18am		
				68 pass-pass
50.3	Worting Jn	pass 11.51am		
				63 pass-stop
83.7	Salisbury	arr 12.23pm	dep 12.28am	
				57 start-pass
122.9	Yeovil Jn	pass 1.9pm		
				58 pass-stop
159.6	Sidmouth Jn	arr 1.47pm	dep 1.51pm	
				60.5 start-pass
170.7	Exmouth Jn	pass 2.2pm		
				22 pass-stop
171.8	Exeter Central	arr 2.5pm	dep 2.21pm	
				12 start-stop
172.4	Exeter St Davids	arr 2.24pm	dep 2.27pm	
				41 start-pass
183.9	Coleford Jn	pass 2.44pm		
				49 pass-stop
190.9	North Tawton	arr 2.55pm	dep 2.56pm	
				32.5 start-stop
197.4	Okehampton	arr 3.8pm	dep 3.14pm	
				20 start-pass
200.1	Meldon Jn	pass 3.22pm		
				35 pass-stop
206.0	Ashbury	arr 3.32pm	dep 3.33pm	
				39 start-stop
209.9	Halwill Jn	arr 3.39pm	dep 3.43pm	
				44 start-stop
215.0	Ashwater	arr 3.50pm	dep 3.51pm	
				36 start-stop
218.6	Tower Hill	arr 3.57pm	dep 3.58pm	
				43 start-stop
223.6	Launceston	arr 4.5pm	dep 4.8pm	
				32 start-stop
227.9	Egloskerry	arr 4.16pm	dep 4.17pm	
				31 start-stop
231.5	Tresmeer	arr 4.24pm	dep 4.25pm	
				33 start-stop
236.4	Otterham	arr 4.34pm	dep 4.35pm	
				38 start-stop
240.8	Camelford	arr 4.42pm	dep 4.43pm	
				29 start-stop
243.2	Delabole	arr 4.48pm	dep 4.49pm	
				35 start-stop
247.3	Port Isaac Road	arr 4.56pm	dep 4.56½pm	
				39 start-stop
249.9	St Kew Highway	arr 5.0½pm	dep 5.1pm	
				35 start-stop
254.0	Wadebridge	arr 5.8pm	dep 5.12pm	
				38 start-stop
259.7	Padstow	arr 5.21pm		

The average speed required from Waterloo to Exeter is 56mph overall, or 58.5mph excluding stops. In contrast, the overall average from Exeter to Padstow of 27mph looks slow, but these figures do not give the whole picture. To run 6½ miles in 12min up a 1 in 77 gradient, even with a light load, calls for a lively engine and practised driving. There are also speed restrictions to be considered; besides local limits there are general limits of 60mph from Waterloo to New Malden and 85mph over the whole Southern Region.

The Salisbury Road

Three trains are scheduled to leave Waterloo on the down main through line: the 10.54am to Salisbury, first stop Woking, 10.57am to Portsmouth, first stop Surbiton, and the 'ACE'. With these close headways, it is essential that trains start on time, so the practice at Waterloo is that if a train does not start by the time the next one is due, it is held back until the next vacant departure path. As cancelling a signalled movement is a complicated business, each train is not signalled until the box is advised, via a call button on each platform, that the train is in fact ready to leave.

The 10.54 is steam-hauled by a 'Lord Nelson' class 4-6-0. After its spectacular departure the 10.57am, comprising four '2-BIL' electric units, moves off quite unobtrusively from Platform 8. Three minutes to go. There is still a commotion of door-banging and whistle-blowing along the train, but up at the front the engine stands quiet and the driver is unconcernedly chatting to a colleague on the platform. Doing things on time, without rushing, has long been second nature to him. He steps on to his footplate, noting that there is no obstruction in front of the engine, the safety valves are beginning to whisper steam at a pressure of 240lb, the handbrake is off and the fireman is checking out of his side of the cab. He opens the small ejector and starts winding his reverser into full forward gear. Through the

Right:
The driver's controls: regulator handle, brake ejector, steam-brake handle, reverser set to 20% cut-off. The large pipe is the vacuum train-pipe and has a cloth covering the mounting of the AWS brake valve which was removed for repair when this 1987 view was taken. *C. Austin*

A perfect spring day in May 1964 sees
No 34066 *Spitfire* halfway up Honiton Bank
with a typical Exeter restaurant car express
with three-coach set No 822 leading. The
lack of smoke shows that the fire is well
burnt through, and she will probably
complete the climb without firing.
Colour-Rail BRS182/the late A. E. Cope

Left:
Starting signals at Waterloo, with multiple-lamp route indicators and subsidiary floodlit signals. WB56 on the left is at Danger, WB59 on the right is cleared to main local.
Courtesy Westinghouse Signals Ltd

train, the faint creak as the brakes release indicates to the observant passenger that the train has come alive and is ready to go. The platform supervisor moves to the parcels lift entrance and presses a plunger labelled 'Ready to Start Platform 10'.

Waterloo's signalmen now begin setting the road. Unnoticed among the tracery of rails, point machines throw their switch blades, locks are engaged and detected, track circuits prove the route is clear. The red signal turns green and the indicator panel lights up with the letters MT — Main Through. The time is 11am. The platform supervisor checks that doors are closed (handles horizontal) and raises his arm in an 'all clear' signal, but he signals to the guard; remember, the guard is in charge of the train. The guard, disdaining the spluttering from the nearby M7 whose driver is already opening her up so that she leans into the back of the train, breaks out his spotless green flag with a flourish that declares that the whole railway may be going to the dogs but there will be nothing slap-dash about the running of *his* train. The supervisor relays the right-away to *Clan Line's* driver, who sounds his whistle and opens his regulator.

The view ahead immediately vanishes as the steam-chest pressure builds up, steam roaring from the cylinder cocks as *Clan Line* takes the strain on those 440 tons of dead weight. The driver pushes the regulator handle back nearly shut; this seemingly illogical action ensures

that if the driving wheels should slip at this moment, the regulator valve will be unable to deliver a large volume of steam to the cylinders and the slip will quickly die away. There is no surge or jerk to be felt by the passengers, but the driver, with hands and feet on his engine's pulse, is the first to know that she has got hold of her load. Very gently, the 'Atlantic Coast Express' starts to move.

To lift a big train over the hump outside Waterloo requires a strong but delicately controlled pull. The torque from the cylinders trying to rotate the engine wheels forwards produces a reaction trying to rotate the engine herself backwards, which has the effect of transferring some of the weight on to the trailing axle where it is useless for adhesion. This gives engines of this type a reputation for being light on their feet, and indeed if the driver should impatiently try to urge her forward she certainly will slip, so he leaves her to pick her own way over the pointwork, busying himself with closing the cylinder cocks and bringing the reverser back to 60%. The little 'M7' will continue to push from the rear until she nears the platform end. On our right an electric train clatters out of the Windsor station, pours itself over the complex of trackwork like a mechanical snake and accelerates away. That is the 11am to Kingston. Its passengers are treated to a broadside view of the 'Merchant Navy' getting under way with majestic slowness, the first exhaust beats coughing out of her chimney and erupting into a great grey-white fountain, gradually but steadily speeding up as the coaches follow her over the hump on to the down main through. There is yet another 11am departure overtaking us on our left; a suburban train to Shepperton running on the down main local. This spectacle of three trains booked to leave a station in the same direction at the same time would be hailed as extraordinary anywhere else: at Waterloo it happens every half hour.

On *Clan Line* the driver is looking for the second of the 35 signals he has to observe in the first 13½ miles to Hampton Court Jn. As the AWS bell rings he pulls the regulator handle open a little wider and winds the reverser to 50%. *Clan Line* pitches and bounces over the West Crossings and continues her seemingly leisurely acceleration. The exhaust beat is now audible above the other noises in the cab, but only just. She seems to be taking the job pretty casually, but the driver is not concerned; he has no intention of thrashing his engine away before she is warmed up merely in order to create an impression, and in any case he knows that, ahead at Loco Junction, the engine for the 11.30 Bournemouth is coming off shed across his path, which could check us if the Eastleigh driver is a little slow off the mark. Sure enough, signal WA14, an automatic three-aspect, is showing yellow and clears to green only as we reach it while WA22, the Vauxhall station starter, is still at one yellow. The driver is prepared to pass it at normal speed because he will then have nearly half a mile in which to stop, so he reduces the cut-off to 35% but keeps steam on her as we approach Vauxhall station, travelling at about 30mph. Moments later WA22 changes to green. He opens the regulator to about halfway. Steam-chest pressure climbs to around 150-160lb and there is a sensation, not discerned by any specific sense, impossible to describe but marvellous to experience, of immense power being released.

During these few minutes the fireman has not been idle. While the driver is looking ahead, it is his job to look back and check that the train is coming along all right and the guard is aboard. He also looks out ahead, as he will do throughout the run when he is not busy, and keeps an eye on the pressure gauge. The start pulls the pressure and boiler water level down sharply, but pressure rises again, indicating that the fire is burning through, so as we approach Vauxhall he starts one injector, opening the steam valve and cutting the water valve back fine. As soon as he sees we have a clear road he opens the fire doors. The fire looks very different now from when we last saw it; at first glance it appears to be nothing but a huge white light with a searing blast of heat to match. The fireman looks at it quite calmly. He pokes the shovel blade, inverted, in the firehole, deflecting the flames so he can see that the fire is burning all over, then he fires a dozen or so shovelfuls: two in each back corner, four across the middle and the rest with a good swing down to the front. The firelight may be seen to be flickering at a rapid tempo, rising quickly because *Clan Line* is leaping ahead and is already doing 50mph. Running over the Queens Road crossover at this speed she bounces violently, which the fireman, standing steadily in the cab centre, does not notice at all. She is not allowed to continue for long, however, as by the Clapham carriage washer the driver knocks the blower valve open and shuts the regulator. At the same time the fireman opens the injector fully to keep her quiet as she coasts down to 40mph at Clapham Junction platforms, 7½min after leaving Waterloo.

The ex-LSWR system differs from the other routes out of London in that the first two miles, including the whole of Waterloo station, is raised on a viaduct, followed by two miles on an embankment, giving splendid views of London, starting with the Palace of Westminster. It is difficult for the passenger to imagine that the wide sweep away from the river originally took the railway clear of the Vauxhall Pleasure Gardens, a favourite out-of-town resort for fashionable Londoners. It is easier to remember the recent past as we look down into backstreets still showing evidence of war damage. This is non-tourist London; battered and shabby it may look, but it cradled the Londoners whose resilient character was affectionately captured by Ealing Film Studios in their tale *Passport to Pimlico* (Pimlico is on the far side of Vauxhall bridge, but location scenes for the film were on this side, right beside the railway). Nowadays a new, go-getting, high-rise image of London is thrusting up, typified by the huge Shell office complex which is cutting Waterloo off from the river view.

So far *Clan Line* has emitted little noise of the sort the layman attributes to steam power; but now, at full regulator and 30% cut off, she makes her voice heard. The song of the steam locomotive is the most stirring and exciting music ever created, the more so because it owes nothing to self-conscious art but is a product of power and movement. On a Bulleid Pacific the exhaust beat emerges as a muffled thump at low speeds, merging into a rasping

Right:
On 18 April 1964,
No 35016 *Elders Fyffes*
had a headboard as she
took the 'ACE' away past
Ditchampton. The duty
number, No 6, is pasted on
the top disc. *H. Ballantyne*

Below:
The Ilfracombe portion of
the 'ACE' passing Colleton
Mills in August 1963, on
part of the line that was
never doubled. Close
inspection of this view
shows that the coal is
steaming after a sluice
from the tender spray on
No 34065 *Hurricane*.
Colour-Rail-
BRS504/P. W. Gray

Above:
Launceston station in June 1958, with No 34061 _73 Squadron_ at the down platform. The water column is to the right of the engine, and the signalbox is in the left background. The Launceston-Egloskerry tablet instruments may still be seen, preserved in the museum of the Launceston Steam Railway.
Colour-Rail BRS342/T. B. Owen

Below:
The up 'ACE' has the road out of Padstow at 9.33am on a July morning in 1959. The locomotive, No 34036 _Westward Ho_, is not yet rebuilt. The station house and the Metropole Hotel are visible above the train.
Colour-Rail BRS325/the late A. E. Cope

chatter and crisping up into an exhilarating crackle as the machine warms up and the superheater becomes effective. To the crew it sounds as a hollow cough in the firebox. Never very loud, it is almost obscured at speed by the thumps of the big-ends, the roar of steel tyres on steel rails, the hissing from the brake ejector, the high-pitched note of the injectors and the myriad clatters and rattles of 150tons of machinery proceeding at a mile a minute. A veritable orchestra of sounds is produced, at a crescendo level if you are in the middle of it: but years of daily experience give the driver a tuned ear that can not only detect anything out of the ordinary but gives him a sense of how hard his engine is working. On a 'Merchant Navy' he is provided with a speedometer, a steam-chest pressure gauge and an illuminated reverser scale, but even without these aids he can still run to time and work his engine in the most economical way by driving according to what he hears and feels. Thus the locomotive talks to the driver; not, perhaps, in the anthropomorphic manner of those in children's story books, but none the less in a very real and important way.

As we head into Clapham cutting, the fireman resumes feeding his fire, as he will do at frequent intervals for the next hour. In order to fire from the right side of the cab, he has to work, as some people would see it, left-handed, with his left hand on the T-handle of the shovel and his right hand down near the blade. Standing just right of cab centre, he fills the shovel and turns to his right to the firehole. (Some drivers used to believe this was because it was disrespectful of a fireman to turn his back on his driver.) The length of the cab is such that he can swing round, moving only one foot, and send his shovelful into the fire in one movement. The height of the tender shovelling-plate is also important in minimising the labour of firing. It is comparatively simple, moving in this fashion, to pull a shovelful round into the right hand corner of the fire, but getting it over to the left is more difficult. To ensure that it goes into the back corner, just in front of where the driver is sitting, he may bring the heel of the shovel hard on to the right-hand side of the firehole and use the latter as a fulcrum to lever the coal round, or, if his wrists are strong enough, another technique is to take an overhand grip with the left hand and flick the shovel over to the left. Most of the coal is put into the back corners of the box and down the sides, for on a 'Merchant Navy' the fire should be flat or slightly saucer-shaped, sloping from back to front. Gravity will help to roll coal to the front

assisted by a slight slope on the grate, although some should be thrown down to prevent it getting too thin. This bending and turning with a loaded shovel puts stress on the chest, stomach and lower back as well as the arms; to keep it up for several hours every day requires a fit man.

Clapham Cutting is so big and has been here for so long, it is easy to forget that it was dug by hand, with picks and spades. Ahead of us the Shepperton train is accelerating from its Clapham Junction stop and gradually matches our speed until the two are running side by side at about 45mph. Passengers in the electric train always look up as a steam locomotive draws alongside, to watch the interplay of piston and valve rods, the bursts of black lacing the white exhaust as her fireman applies another 'round'. After a couple of minutes the 'Juice' train drops behind, as it stops at Earlsfield. The view hereabouts, as we gain another embankment, is a pretty uninspiring townscape, but it must have looked different in 1803 when the first public railway in the world, the Surrey Iron Railway, was opened from Wandsworth to Croydon. A small tunnel passes under Earlsfield station platforms and is widely supposed, logically if not evidentially, to be the site at least of this pioneering railway.

A steam locomotive is a creature of ever-changing balances; or as the scientific mind would see it, a dynamic equilibrium between several variables. Boiler pressure, boiler water level, fire thickness, fire temperature and steam consumption are inter-related. Adding feed-water to the boiler will reduce the pressure, a bigger fire produces more heat but takes longer to rise in temperature, using more steam increases the draught on the fire and makes it burn faster but also uses more water. To complicate the issue, opening the regulator causes the water level to rise in the gauge-glass, the water expands with a rise in temperature, the firebox contains a brick arch which acts as a heat reservoir and introduces a pronounced hysteresis effect in the response of the boiler. The fireman is in command of this system; his tools are a shovel to add coal, injectors to add water, dampers to reduce draught on the fire and blower to increase it.

When firing you have always to think ahead. The workload ahead for the engine determines the size of fire you must build, but the bigger the fire the longer you will take to get it into the box and ignited. A demand for a short burst of high power can be met by using the energy stored in the boiler, in which case the water level will fall and the fire will burn away. That is a situation that cannot last beyond a few minutes, so for a longer spell of hard pulling you must add coal and water at the rate the driver is consuming them. However, when you have got things going at a high steaming rate, there will come a time when it has to stop. You must anticipate that and run down the fire or water level so that when the demand for steam ceases you can divert your heat reserves into igniting a fresh charge of coal or boiling an extra intake of water.

What cannot be foreseen is the unscheduled stop. All that can be done then is to fill the boiler; if the delay is very long the fire may be raked back into a heap to reduce its rate of burning, but when these measures are complete the engine will just have to lose any remaining surplus energy by lifting her safety valves. This is a total waste of fuel. Stopping a steam train unexpectedly is thus an expensive business which signalmen are exhorted to avoid as far as possible. Even worse, for the fireman, is the opposite, a demand for steam for which you are not ready. Fortunately the 'MN' boiler will cope with this. If you start building up the fire and the driver opens her up to put a strong draught through the fire, it will make more steam than the cylinders are using. And the faster and harder she goes, the more steam passes through the cylinders and up the chimney, the more air is drawn through the fire, the faster it burns, the more steam it produces and so on. The exhaust blast becomes formidable at speed; it is quite capable of sucking solid objects like firing shovels through the firehole, and eventually can start lifting small coal from the grate and throwing it out of the chimney. When that happens you have reached the limit of continuous power output.

To work a steam train thus requires knowledge of the route, interpretation of your schedule and teamwork with your driver. Above all, you must be mentally one jump ahead of your engine and keep on top of her, for if you do not she will get on top of you.

From Waterloo to West London Junction the line tends slightly downhill, but from there it turns to a gradual climb which extends with only a few short breaks for the next 50 miles. However, *Clan Line* continues to accelerate although the driver brings the cut-off back to 25%. The superheater is beginning to work. She surges ahead with the eagerness which characterises a good engine, and speed reaches 60mph. Approaching Wimbledon we pass on our right Durnsford Road power station and the big sheds of Wimbledon Park electric train depot. The first electric services on South Western tracks were those of the District Railway to Wimbledon in 1905. Durns-

Below:
The view west from Durnsford Road: down local, up local coming over its flyover and vanishing behind signal WH130, down through, up through with a Salisbury-Waterloo train hauled by No 34066 *Spitfire*, Railway Staff Halt and Wimbledon Park carriage shed. *R. Fisher*

Right:
The glorious return of steam in the autumn of 1986 gave the opportunity for this footplate view from *Clan Line*, approaching Buckhorn Weston Tunnel in the up direction on the now-singled main line. Prominent on the boilerside are the well-polished feedwater delivery pipes.
T. C. Robbins

Right:
Was this really the last steam train at Waterloo? On 1 October 1988 *Clan Line* was displayed, in steam but stationary, for the Ian Allan Network Day. MNLPS staff are seen putting up the reproduction headboard, which she later carried down the main line to Basingstoke. *Hugh Madgin*

ford Road started generating in 1915 for the first electrics out of Waterloo on 25 October. By the close of 1916 the LSWR suburban system was all electric, with the third rail extending to Hampton Court Junction on the main line. The mainline scheme of 1936-37 took it as far as Pirbright Junction when trains began running to Farnham in January 1937. Crews working steam engines on electrified tracks are supposed to minimise use of sand, avoid dropping water or ash on the track, not to put fire-irons out of the cab and of course be extremely careful if they have to get off the engine.

At Wimbledon we pass under a concrete flyover, built during the 1936 resignalling, which carries the up local line over both through lines. The LSWR was the first company to exploit the flying junction as a means of increasing traffic flow, at Twickenham in 1882. We pass flyovers (or dive-unders) for branch lines at Raynes Park, New Malden, Hampton Court, Byfleet, Pirbright, Sturt Lane, Worting and Amesbury Junctions. Through Wimbledon station, past the long milk dock on the right, and we are on a level stretch, on an embankment across the valley of the Beverley Brook and Hogsmill River. The passengers may now feel they are in the country, with Carters Seeds grounds on the left and the Southern Railway playing fields on the right,

just before a singularly unlovely bridge carrying the Kingston By-pass.

By now the fireman will have a good idea of how well the engine is steaming. If she is doing badly he would have to take extra care to keep a bright fire and perhaps allow the water level to fall in anticipation of four short respites where the driver could ease her to give him a chance to recover: from Surbiton to Hampton Court Junction, from Weybridge to Byfleet, a short drop near Sturt Lane and about a mile down beyond Hook. If she is percolating well he adjusts the injector to keep the water level an inch below the top of the glass and sets the back damper about half open. The driver pulls her up slightly to about 22% and may even ease the regulator down to check the speed; there is a limit of 60mph as far as New Malden and we are already doing a good 65mph. As Berrylands station (erected in 1933 beside a large sewage works) flashes by, signal WA70, an automatic colour-light, is caught in the act of changing from double yellow to green,

Below:
No 35012 *United States Lines* passing signal WA70 on 15 February 1958. Signal WA72, showing double yellow, is for the local line; the striped box contains a telephone.
D. Herman

because the 10.57 ahead of us has slowed to cross over to the local line for its first stop at Surbiton.

Surbiton station is approached through a huge cutting which reminds us of the expense railway companies had to incur in placating powerful landowners through whose territory they sought to pass. It could have been avoided by routeing the line slightly to the North, but that would have meant entering the ancient and royal borough of Kingston, which would have no truck with the railway at any price. So the company hid Kingston station in the cutting and waited for the inevitable shift in focus from the old town, which happened so fast that by 1869 Kingston was overjoyed to be given just a branch line. The present Surbiton station was completely rebuilt in 1937 to the designs of the Southern Railway architect J. R. Scott. It was intended to be the best of everything modern; a gleaming white palace of progress and a model for the future (a future that did not of course include nasty, dirty steam trains). Whether you regard it as a pity or a relief that the war intervened and made Surbiton not the first but the last big station to be given this treatment, is perhaps a matter of taste; 20 years of weather and air pollution have made the sugar-cube building less enticing. The 'ACE' whistles through the middle of it at 70mph.

The engineman seldom thinks in terms of speed, as such. To him the railway is divided into parcels of time. Hampton Court Junction is a scheduled timing point at 11.18am, the next is Worting Junction at 11.51am. The former is also the end of the colour-light signals. The next box, Esher East, is a mechanical interlock-

Above:
Fred Prickett driving No 35019 *French Line CGT* in the mid-1960s. These views were taken when the crew took a camera to work on an ordinary day. *MNLPS*

Below:
No 35019's young fireman attends to his fire, screwing up his eyes against the brilliant white light. *MNLPS*

ing frame whose points and signals are driven by air at a pressure of 10lb/sq in and whose links to its neighbours include the Sykes Lock-and-Block System. This is an attempt to render the block section impregnable by locking each starting signal electrically from the box ahead so that once it has been pulled off to admit a train to the section, it cannot be pulled again until the train has passed through a track circuit at the far end of the section. The combination of electric, pneumatic and mechanical seems a rather unholy alliance, but it made the best use of technology available in 1902 when Sir Sam Fay brought the idea of automatic powered signalling over from America. Esher was one of the original London & Southampton Railway stations, opened on 21 May 1838 to serve a genteel district including Sandown Park racecourse, whereas Hersham is the newest station on the route, opened on 28 September 1936.

The built-up area ends around Hampton Court Junction. When the Southern Railway published its *Southern Rambles for Londoners* it needed go no further than the common by Esher station to photograph a rambler posed in the countryside, and the spot is still the same today. From a long embankment across the Mole Valley we run through Walton-on-Thames and into a very broad cutting through a ridge of hill which separates the River Mole from the River Wey. A long blast on the whistle is required before Walton as a safety measure, for the 10.57 Portsmouth train is just pulling away on the down local line. We are still about half a minute behind schedule as a result of the two slight checks on our way out of London,

but going well at 73mph. There is a swirl of turbulent air as *Clan Line* bores her way between the 10.57am on her left and the 9.34am Portsmouth-Waterloo passing on her right.

Two very long sidings on the up side extend from Walton to the delightfully secluded box at Oatlands, which basks in its sheltered valley with just a couple of crossovers to look after. They contain an assortment of carriages, overflows from Clapham Junction and part of the capital stock that only earns a return on summer weekends. Beyond Weybridge station the view changes again into another embankment vista, this time of watermeadows on the right and Brooklands on the left. Some parts of the Brooklands racetrack are still in place, including a long piece close beside the railway. Built in 1907 this was the first purpose-built car-racing track in the world, and the ground it enclosed was the cradle of the English aircraft industry. Now it is Vickers of

Below:
Byfleet Junction with No 34090 *Sir Eustace Missenden, Southern Railway* on the down through. The signals above her standing clear are for the up through. The down signals are behind the signalbox, to the right of which is the down line from Addlestone. *MNLPS*

Above:
No 35021 *New Zealand Line* under the automatic signal gantry between Pirbright and Sturt Lane, where only the local lines are electrified. The train is up from Weymouth, on 16 September 1960. The number 786 on the end coach is a set number for the first three coaches. *MNLPS/The late Derek Cross*

Weybridge. Here we may catch a glimpse of the prototype of the new wonder jet airliner, the VC10, looking much too big to get off the ground in the space where Lord Trenchard learnt to fly. Byfleet Junction signals can be seen in the distance, the through line signals standing clear and the local line signals at danger, signifying that the 10.54 Salisbury is on the local out of our way, having been switched over at Esher, Walton or Weybridge. Also in the distance a steam train comes into sight travelling at speed on the up through. This is the 9.22am from Bournemouth. Two minutes later another steam train, the 8.35am from Bournemouth, comes up on the local.

The driver now resets the regulator to produce a slightly higher reading on the steam chest pressure gauge, in acknowledgement of the adverse gradient and a southerly wind which has blown the clouds away. Crosswinds, sneaking into the gaps between and beneath coaches, put more resistance on a train than the head-winds which prevail on this route. A considerate driver alters the controls infrequently on a long run so as to sustain a steady demand for steam, making matters simpler for the fireman. The latter is constantly active now: firing a dozen shovelfuls, breaking a big lump of coal, adjusting the injector, checking the boiler water gauge, sweeping up with a handbrush damped in the bucket, firing another 'round'. He makes a point of seeing as many signals as possible; at Hampton Court Junction and Esher distant he will get a view of the signal before the driver does and raises his left hand, palm open, with a shout of 'Right'. Apart from that there is virtually no conversation between the two. For one thing, it is too noisy: for another, each man trusts the other

as a professional to do his job. There is no let-up. The engine roars on steadily, demanding unceasing vigilance and attention. Speed falls gradually to a steady 68mph, boiler pressure 240lb/sq in, water level an inch below the top nut.

On the approach to Woking there are three prominent buildings on the left. The factory is the works of James Walker Ltd, makers of packings, jointings and steam plant accessories. The mosque was built before World War 2 by an Englishman who became an enthusiast for Oriental customs. The big house is the Southern Railwaymen's Home for Children.

The Woking Homes form one of the best known railway charities. They started in 1886 when a house in Jeffrey's Road, Clapham, was bought as an orphanage for children of deceased or distressed railway employees. The present building opened in 1909. It was financed and managed on a voluntary basis by railwaymen. Since World War 2 the demand for housing children has fallen and the Home now also cares for retired people from the transport industry.

Woking station was rebuilt in 1937 to accommodate the increased traffic created by the Portsmouth electrification. The signalbox is clearly a relative of those at Wimbledon and contains Westinghouse equipment. Its occupants have a busy life, as the junction of the

Above:
On this West of England express near Sturt Lane in August 1960 the first three coaches are to Maunsell's design, Nos 3771, 3788 and 5654. Locomotive No 35020 *Bibby Line*. *The late Derek Cross*

main and Portsmouth lines is on the level, and many a summer extra boat train has ground to a halt between here and Brookwood, engine blowing off furiously, because a 'Pompey' is being crossed in front of it. A curiosity at the junction is that the down local line is diverted round an insignificant-looking hut in a generous double S-bend. The 10.54 is negotiating this curve at the moment when the 'ACE' overtakes it, possibly giving some passengers an instant of panic belief that they are about to be carried to Portsmouth.

Beyond Woking there is no electric third rail beneath us, and no more colour-light signals. The local lines are electrified as far as Sturt Lane Junction, but are normally only used by the Alton electrics which branch off at Pirbright Junction. As far as the Basingstoke approaches, trains are controlled by automatic signals installed by the LSWR in 1912. They are actuated by the low-pressure air system. A main airpipe runs the length of the line connecting a system of air receivers with pump installations at Fleet and Basingstoke. At the latter are four big air receivers, a main diesel compressor and a standby steam unit with two old locomotive boilers. All main line points in the Basingstoke area are also air-operated. The signals have standard LSWR lower quadrant arms mounted on gantries at intervals of one mile. They are placed above the centre-lines of the tracks, which is inconvenient as the nearer one gets to them the more they are obscured

by steam from one's engine. On a damp day a driver on an original Bulleid Pacific, with low-pressure exhaust steam flopping out of the chimney and hanging about in front of him, can experience considerable difficulty, and in bad conditions he might have to shut off steam in order to see a signal. Although he has the bell of the AWS, he is still required to see the signal arm or light itself. There is only one action if you miss seeing a signal; stop.

The driver decides a little more power is needed so he sets her down to 25% and 180lb on the steam chest. This railway was built according to George Stephenson's dictum that the gradient on a main line should not exceed 1 in 330. To observe it the earthworks are on a gigantic scale, and we are entering the biggest excavation of all, Deepcut. The three-arch bridge carries a minor road 55ft above us. It marks the end, at Milepost 31, of the continuous gradient. The engine is eased to 22% and accelerates. A few yards to the north of us, the Basingstoke Canal, which we have been following from Byfleet, passes through its own cutting and turns south to cross over the railway — or rather the railway crosses it, for it was there first. In order to support the weight of puddled clay containing the canal on masonry arches, the arches are of minimum size, forming in effect four short single-line tunnels. The fireman shuts the firedoors and turns on the blower. The driver draws his sliding side window over. Both men close their eyes.

Whump!

Down into Farnborough, with more views across heathland and pine woods much of which is owned by the War Office; Aldershot lies to the left and Sandhurst to the right. The

fireman pauses in his labours to replace 35min worth of sweat with a cup of tea, while he watches the road through the station. The engine chooses the perfect moment to kick her tail violently sideways and straighten out with two or three wriggles, thus slopping the precious tea down the chin and giving rise to the comment, extensively used in steam operating practice, that is best expressed in print as '* * * *'.

Between Sturt Lane and Farnborough we cross over the River Blackwater, which marks the boundary between Surrey and Hampshire. Hereabouts is another point where, if everything is running precisely to time, a lineside watcher stands a chance of seeing three steam trains pass in close succession if not at once. The 11.10am stopper up from Basingstoke is due to call at Farnborough at 11.37am, about the same time as the 9.3am from Templecombe passes through on the up and the 'ACE' on the down.

There is also a possibility of seeing a goods train. The London area is so saturated with passenger trains that most freight movements take place only at night, but as we head west the traffic thins out past each junction: so making available more paths in the timetable. Although the Southern lines are traditionally passenger lines with a proportion of goods to passenger vehicles about half that of other railways, their freight traffic is not inconsiderable. The major flow in the South Western London division is between Feltham marshalling yard and Southampton, via Byfleet Junction and Basingstoke. Woking Up Yard will be busy, as it is the focal point for the permanent way engineers' activities, where ballast from Meldon Quarry, sleepers from Redbridge and rails from Stoke are assembled

for their weekend forays. Farnborough forwards wagons for the Royal Aircraft Establishment, which advanced scientific emporium maintains its own railway. The highly polished little saddle tank *Invincible* makes her way through the streets, her main cargo being coal for the boiler house. Newnham Siding is a depot for the Hook brickworks.

The line on which *Clan Line* is travelling at a steady 75mph runs straight and level over Bramshott Heath, and it is just too bad that Fleet Pond, the largest lake south of the Thames, happens to be in the way. Locke's navvies cut off the north end of it by building a sand bank retained in a timber frame, facing it with a layer of chalk.

As we pass the old village of Basing, and Barton Mill on the River Lodden, Basingstoke distant signal comes into view. It is off, but the driver closes down the regulator until only 20lb/sq in is indicated on the steam-chest gauge, in order to slow down for a 65mph speed limit through Basingstoke. He catches the fireman's eye and makes a spreading gesture, which the latter interprets correctly as meaning that the firedoors should be opened as he has a big fire in her and rather a lot of smoke is coming from the chimney. He opens the blower slightly as well, and starts the front injector. Basingstoke is not the commuter centre it will become in the electric era with a train every 10min in the rush hour, but it enjoys an approximately half-hourly service to London. A plume of steam in the carriage sidings on our right shows where an engine is being attached to the empty stock of the 12.12pm. The fireman moves into his seat, holding the frame of the open sliding window beside him with a cloth in his hand, as a branch line from Reading comes in on the right. The engine rides the crossings well but the tender, with no tension on its couplings to steady it, pitches quite wickedly. Then we are through the platforms and the driver is opening her up to nearly full regulator and 30% to maintain 60mph. The boiler pressure, which was down at 200lb/sq in before the Basingstoke slack, is 220lb; the front injector is shut off and even though the back one is still on and the engine is accelerating uphill, she continues to come round to about 235lb/sq in at Worting and 240lb/sq in by Oakley, so the fireman is well pleased with the result of his efforts and contents himself with a couple of rounds in the back corners and sides on the way to the summit.

Worting is an important point on the line, as it is where the Bournemouth and West of England lines diverge. The line which so far

Above:
At Worting box, No 35018 *British India Line*, coasting with regulator shut and blower cracked, is slowing to cross from the down through to the down Bournemouth. Beyond the bridge, the left-hand junction signal is off. *MNLPS*

Below:
The West of England line at Battledown flyover, with an 'S15' on an up train. *MNLPS*

has been the down local becomes the down Bournemouth line, and similarly the up Bournemouth line comes over a flyover and becomes the up local, so at Worting cross-overs, laid out with half-mile radius points that can be taken comfortably at 50mph, are provided to rearrange trains on to their proper roads. For us there is no restriction, we go straight through and soon *Clan Line* leans into the curve under Battledown bridge. The summit of the long gradual rise from London is in a cutting a mile beyond Oakley station; here the driver pulls her up to 25% and eases the regulator back to about two-thirds open. Speed rises gradually but steadily to 70mph at Overton (if you want to forge £1 notes, the paper mill here uses water from the newly-sprung River Test to make the paper on which they are printed), 75mph at Whitchurch, where that impudent intruder, the Didcot, Newbury & Southampton Railway, crosses over, and 80mph on the high viaduct at Hurstbourne. Oakley summit is not high as summits go, only 400ft, but the airy chalk downs look and smell totally different from the Thames Valley landscape.

'We seldom ran at less than 20% cut-off. Anything less made you unpopular with the fireman on an 'MN', and, as the older drivers would put it, it was better to give them a bit of freedom round the front.' *A. E. Hooker*

Besides noise and heat, *Clan Line* subjects her occupants to a thorough shaking. With such a concentration of weight sitting on 18 wheels it

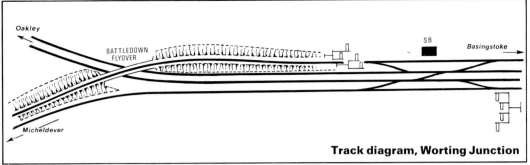

could not be otherwise, although Bulleid 4-6-2s ride as well as any. Their secret is in the '-2', a swinging rear truck whose pivot is 3ft behind the rear coupled axle. It has powerful side-control springs and holds the back end very steady. The even turning moment of three cylinders virtually eliminates the usual tendency of steam engines to nose from side to side, but since it is impossible to make three things exactly the same there is bound to be a slight residual imbalance. The middle cylinder is inclined at $7\frac{1}{2}°$ so the forces in it have a vertical component. The result is that when working very hard at low speed a circular motion is sometimes felt on the footplate. It may be reinforced by lurches induced by track irregularities, and if the natural period of sideways oscillation, which is rather less than a second, is picked up a pretty violent swing can occur. Pitching is minimal and she is unlikely to lift your feet off the floor. The rotating coupling rods are balanced by weights on the wheels, but the various masses are moving in different planes, causing forces perpendicular to the axles which are known as 'hammer-blow'. To them are added a vibration from steam pushing the pistons, giving six impacts per wheel revolution.

The tender has no sophisticated suspension arrangements, in fact it is little better than a six-wheeled wagon. From the train a high-mileage tender on uneven track can be seen banging from side to side in an alarming manner. However, it has a low centre of gravity and does not roll, so a footplate passenger, who is more conscious of the riding qualities than the crew because he has less to occupy his mind, may well find it preferable to stand on the tender front and watch the engine dance about in front of him.

An hour after starting, the train is sweeping down towards Andover Junction at 85mph. From a high embankment we see the town of Andover with its prominent church tower a mile away on the left, showing little sign as yet of the expansion destined to turn the sur-

rounding fields into trading estates. The junction serves the branch line to Romsey and is also the southern terminus of the Midland & South Western Junction Railway, a once-independent line which cut straight across the broad-gauge GWR and had the cheek to site its headquarters in the heart of the latter at Swindon! Some say that the Western has been trying ever since to excise this thorn from its flesh; be that as it may, we see no train in the up loop as there are only three per day. What we do see is a line of Lowmac flat wagons loaded with tarpaulin-shrouded vehicles of some uncertain sort. They are bound to or from Tidworth Camp, the eastern end of the vast military complex on Salisbury Plain. The Army presence in this area began in 1897 with a purchase of 750 acres of land near the village of Bulford. Today it extends from Ludgershall to Warminster, an area 24 miles by seven miles in which every military evolution is tested. It reached its peak in 1943 when exercises entailed taking over the main line between Grateley and Porton for trying rail-borne artillery, but it is still very active today. As we climb towards Grateley summit a strange arrow-shaped aeroplane is seen overhead; an English Electric Lightning, the very latest in jet fighters, preparing to land at Boscombe Down airfield.

On the 1 in 178 descent *Clan Line* is running with part regulator and 22% cut-off, so the fireman is able to sit down for a few minutes and catch Andover Junction distant, which is visible on his side first. As she hurtles through the station the driver gives her full regulator at 25% and she goes up the four-track section to Red Post Junction (the other two tracks are the MSWJ) with little drop in speed and reaches about 87mph in the dip beyond. At this speed her exhaust beat sounds like a continuous ripple which itself is drowned in a sudden roar as pressure reaches 250lb/sq in and a safety valve lifts. To blow off against an injector whilst working uphill is no small feat, so the fireman doffs his cap and makes an elegant

57

bow to the driver, who grins and snicks the reverser ahead another notch. The noise continues for 20sec, seeming longer, then ceases; pressure falls on the climb through Grateley to about 220lb/sq in and once over the top the injector goes on full to keep it there. During the run down past Amesbury Junction and Porton the fireman carries out a boiler blowdown. (This is not really necessary since it was done at the shed, but he does not know that.) It is done with the remote-controlled valve, driven by a steam plunger supplied from the manifold through duplicate valves. There is also a timing gauge (note, if you refer to the 'clock' you mean the pressure gauge). He shuts off the injector, turns on the blowdown valve tentatively and immediately turns it off again. Satisfied that it does in fact shut off, he opens it up for 30sec on the gauge. The outflow from the valve is not as violent as that from the manual one and is delivered into a silencing shroud, but even so it fills the cab with steam and one may visualise that it is not doing the permanent way any good. After this we are down to about a third of a glass of water, so the injector goes on full, then, as we have a hot fire and the engine is cruising with only 100lb/sq in on the steam-chest, the second injector is started to fill her up. He builds up the fire in readiness for the next leg of the run. With that vicious white heat blacked out and the firedoors closed it is a little cooler in the cab.

From Grateley to Porton, *Clan Line*, her crew and passengers are following the steps of a mind-stretching number of past wayfarers. Just behind the bushes on our right is the Portway, a road which was ancient when the Romans came. Our chariot rushes through a bridge into Porton station, and dead ahead, 4½ miles away, is the 404ft-high spire of Salisbury Cathedral. A minute later the driver pushes the regulator handle down to reduce steam-chest pressure to 20lb/sq in. After another minute he pulls the brake handle down slightly until a check is felt in our headlong charge towards the approaching spire. He does not expect to be stopped at Salisbury Tunnel Junction but he must of course be ready for it, and it looks as though there has been a rain shower here recently, so the rail might be greasy. We emerge from the last cutting above the meadows of the Bourne with St Thomas's Bridge on our left and he applies a little more brake. The train-pipe vacuum gauge is now showing 13in, giving 7in (about 3½lb/sq in) brake pressure on the leading coaches, slightly less at the rear, being held there by the balance between the brake valve admitting air to the trainpipe and the vacuum ejector trying to suck

it out again. At this level the engine steam brake automatically comes into action. *Clan Line* is fitted with two 8in bore cylinders which look small, but the total force they apply to the brake blocks, 12 in number, in a full-power application is 87 tons. (Since this is more than the weight on the braked wheels, it is possible to lock the wheels at low speeds.) As the blocks come up against the wheel tyres, they first skim off any moisture picked up off the rail. Then they touch, and in the first moment of contact a spray of white-hot particles of iron flies everywhere, to settle on the oily surfaces of wheels, motion, brake rodding, etc. This mixture of iron dust and oil forms a peculiarly tenacious sludge which is a very effective preservative but takes a great deal of cleaning off. At 60 miles an hour the kinetic energy of the 'ACE' is about 5×10^9ft lb, which must all be converted into heat and dissipated to the four winds by the time we stop in Salisbury station. The driver looks over to the fireman. 'All right for the Distant?' Although he cannot see it, he knows exactly when it will be visible. 'Right, it's off, mate.'

He eases the brake application, and at about 50mph she coasts on. Salisbury spire sinks into the city as we approach, to disappear as we reach the curve into Tunnel Junction and the driver checks her again for the 40mph limit. On the left an overgrown embankment can just be seen which once carried a connection to allow direct running to Romsey and Southampton. The junction is immediately in front of Fisherton Tunnel, the first tunnel on our route, 443yd long. The fireman finishes making up his fire, sets the door half-open and opens the blower as we run into the tunnel. It is instantly dark — the only lights on in the cab are those illuminating the water gauges. Little tongues of flame lick out of the firehole, and the fireman resets the blower so as to pull them back in. The general racket is supplemented by a howl from the AWS siren, set off by a distant signal at the far end of the tunnel which is fixed permanently at Caution. The driver cancels it and makes a brake application as we emerge into the built-up area, bringing her down to 10mph as a very sharp right-hand curve comes up. On the down side is Salisbury East box, the

old LSWR box modernised with a flat roof when the electropneumatic system was installed. The installation here is a big one, with a diesel compressor and five air receivers each 8ft by 5ft diameter. On the up side is a marshalling yard in which an S15 class engine is collecting wagons to form the 12.55pm goods to Templecombe. The driver consults his watch. We are about a minute ahead of schedule, having covered the 33 miles from Worting in just over 29min at an average speed of 68mph.

Above:
A very grubby 'M7', No 30025, finishing her days on pilot duty at Salisbury, carrying red and white lamps at each end. Beside her is an electro-pneumatic point machine with a ground disc signal. In the background are a goods shed and part of the old station up platform. *B. J. Lake*

Below:
***Clan Line* entering Salisbury with the LCGB 'Somerset & Dorset' tour on 5 March 1966.**
E. W. J. Crawforth

A Change of Scene

The Salisbury-Exeter road is generally considered to be harder than that from London, owing to the more economical mode adopted in its design. To avoid the stupendous earthworks raised by Giles, the route follows river valleys in miles of curves, and climbs them on a ruling gradient of 1 in 80. When an 11-coach plus 'Merchant Navy' train is placed on a 1 in 80, its weight exerts a force of 6 tons 17cwt down the slope, more than 40% of the maximum tractive force available at low speed. We hope to take all the hills on the run, but should we be stopped at Crewkerne, for example, it would be necessary to re-start on such a gradient.

The railway traverses a series of switchbacks through Wiltshire and Dorset, through unspoilt country of farms and villages which are the true heart and essence of England. The industries of the compact market towns are agriculture-based and go back centuries. Pre-cotton age textiles: the sails of Nelson's *Victory* were made in Crewkerne, Honiton was the market for the Dorset lace industry, and tanning and leatherwork are still carried on by old-established firms such as Dykes of Milborne Port. Gillingham still has its silk mill, glove factory, brewery and the bacon factory of Oake, Woods & Co next door to the station, Axminster and Wilton have their carpet factories. Dairy farming is big business hereabouts; the first depot for supplying London with fresh milk was set up at Semley station in 1871. Chard Junction has a big processing plant and Seaton Junction has the Express Dairy Milk And Egg Depot.

The start from Salisbury is a heavy one right from the platform end, with a reverse curve over three turnouts. As her rear coupled wheels reach the crossing of the first turnout, *Clan Line* slips; a gout of black smoke is torn out of her by the sudden rush of steam and the speedometer, which is a little generator rotated by the wheels, bounces up to 25mph. The driver instantly shuts the regulator, then waits until the shuddering spin has ceased before he pulls over the steam sand handle. The sanders, a species of force-pump sucking sand from the boxes and blowing it at the wheels, come into action with a distinctive spluttering noise, obscuring the wheels in vapour.

She digs her feet in again and pulls away past the GWR signalbox on the right, West box and engine shed on the left. In the yard outside the locomotive depot we may see a 'King Arthur' class 4-6-0, one of those which hauled the Exeter expresses, including the 'ACE', during the interwar years before the 'MNs' arrived, but now relegated to stopping trains and fast freight work.

Our new driver opens her well out fairly quickly and does not link up beyond 35% as she labours up the 1 in 115 towards Wilton. Only three miles from Salisbury centre, Wilton might be thought a mere satellite village, but remember that the county we are in is called Wiltshire. Wilton was the seat of power, the centre with the big house, for some six centuries since Domesday. Salisbury was the upstart, developed as a result of its position on the navigable River Avon, a market centre whose inhabitants owed their position to trade. In 1960 it still has its sheep market and wool warehouse. As Salisbury has blossomed, Wilton has declined and merits only a small station — two small stations, that is. The WR and South Western lines run together in the same cutting from Salisbury, to divide here.

Wilton West station lies a few yards north of Wilton South.

Clan Line works up to 45mph before shutting off for a 40mph limit on the curve through Wilton South. The fireman fires a round and turns an injector on for a short time.

The acceleration downhill past Ditchampton School is quite remarkable. The river we cross is the Wylye, which the GWR line follows; we head up the valley of the Nadder, over the watershed at Semley Common and off on a rollercoaster ride across two valleys, the Stour and the Cale. Between Dinton and Semley the route is a succession of curves. Coming the other way they look very sharp as you get up to 80mph or so, but the track is so superbly aligned that the engine swings into each one in a sinuous flow. The down train blasts along at 50-55mph, reaching 65mph on a level stretch beyond Dinton. Midway between Dinton and Tisbury Quarry we pass a siding, curving off into the hills, which you will not find on any map. It leads to Chilmark, a top-secret military depot dug into disused chalk workings. Connections to military establishments appear all over the South Western; it has more associations with the armed services than any other railway company. Dinton's quiet station was during World War 1 the railhead for a huge camp at Fovant, housing troops from the dominions. It was the troops who carved the regimental badges seen on the chalk down below Chiselbury Ring.

Halfway up the final pitch to Semley summit the line passes under a bridge on a left-hand curve, and this point is 100 miles from Waterloo. It has taken 105min to reach here, including the stop at Salisbury. *Clan Line* goes over the top at 53mph, with pressure down to 210lb sq in but the water out of sight at the top of the glass. The reason for this is evident when she noses over on to a 1 in 100 down and the driver eases her to half regulator, for the water abruptly drops a good 2in. The fireman continues to feed his fire until he has a slight black mound in front of the doors, and again puts an injector on, leaves the doors ajar and knocks the blower on to clear the smoke as the driver pulls her up to 17% and the blast on the fire subsides. Pressure quickly comes round to the mark again while speed increases by 30mph in a couple of miles. At a steady 85mph we round a bend and see ahead a road overbridge at Gillingham station, looking from up here much too small for *Clan Line* to dive beneath it. There is a pronounced surge back on the drawbar as we go through the station.

Between Salisbury and Exeter we should pass several up trains, which are as follows:

At Tisbury Quarry, the 12.00pm Templecombe-Salisbury goods.

At Gillingham, the 12.43pm Templecombe-Salisbury passenger, just drawing in.

At Sherborne, the 8.55am Ilfracombe-Waterloo Near Hewish Crossing, the up Atlantic Coast Express.

At Whitford (near Seaton Junction), the 11.10am Plymouth-Brighton.

After Honiton, the 1.10pm Exeter-Salisbury.

During our Sidmouth Junction stop, the 1.25pm Exmouth Junction-Salisbury goods.

Near Broad Clyst, an 'M7' class engine running light, on its way up to Honiton to act as pilot there.

At Whipton in Exeter suburbs, a trip goods going up to Pinhoe before shunting out the local private sidings.

During this period, around midday, the down line is not particularly busy, and one reason for this is the need to keep it clear for the high-speed passage of the 'ACE'. Only two stations, Yeovil Junction and Seaton Junction, have running loops where one train may overtake another. When we leave Salisbury the stopping train conveying our last coach starts only 8min behind us, but it reaches Yeovil Junction 40min after we do and no other traffic can utilise the gap. Meanwhile, we are rapidly overhauling the 11.45am Yeovil-Exeter, which in turn must hit a path between the intensive Exmouth-Exeter services. All this means that the residents of Crewkerne, for instance, have no train to Exeter between 12.18pm and 2.10pm.

From Gillingham we climb away from the River Stour to a tunnel, 742yd long, under a ridge on which Sandley House is a prominent landmark. The tunnel is named after the nearest village, Buckhorn Weston. Like Honiton further west, it has suffered from water ingress, but two years ago its brick lining was rebuilt and we can now go through at full speed in the dry. The driver does not alter his control settings, with a good maximum speed and a free-steaming engine there is no need. The kinetic energy the train loses in slowing from 80mph to 65mph provides the work to lift it up the incline. This is an example of the switchback theory of railway design in operation, but of course it only works if high speeds are permissible in the 'dips' and is no help at all to someone who has stopped at Gillingham.

Buckhorn Weston summit, at milepost 107½ just outside the tunnel, is spectacular because the gradient switches from 1 in 100 up to 1 in 100 down in a few yards. A train going over it can be seen describing a quite noticeable vertical curve.

To make our passage of the tunnel more comfortable the regulator is eased and the blower turned on. The blower is put on whenever entering a tunnel, as the sudden interpolation of a roof a few feet above our chimney interrupts the exhaust stream and could partially destroy the smokebox vacuum; fast-burning gas from the fire might then swirl out through the firehole. Through the tunnel, we have a superb straight run across the Blackmoor Vale. The fireman pauses from his labours for a few minutes to enjoy the tremendous surge of acceleration to 85mph, across the little River Cale at Abbey Ford (there is no abbey there now) and up a long embankment. The driver beckons the fireman over.

'How are you doing, boy, do you want a blow?' 'Yeah, we're doing fine. I'll have a blow, though.' He hangs on the whistle cord and sends the Bulleid whistle resounding over the vale, to announce our approach to Templecombe.

Why is Templecombe held to epitomise the railways' custom of indulging in inexplicable processes in the middle of nowhere? To start with, it is hardly fair to call 'nowhere' the attractive twin villages of Templecombe and Abbas Combe, one each side of us, and the many prosperous farms round about; but the source of the 'strange rites' of the poet is the intersection with the Somerset and Dorset Railway. The latter passes under the main line and is connected to it by a steep, sharp curve. There is a short platform on the S&D, but to permit cross-platform changes, trains are backed into (or out of) the main station via this curve. There is also an exchange of goods between the two lines. Most main line goods trains call for remarshalling, crew change or engine change, and because it is halfway between Waterloo and Plymouth, Templecombe was for many years an engine change point for passenger trains as well. However, though it is a well-established employer and district crossroads, the station itself looks totally out of place. It looks like half of Woking station, red-brick, concrete and all, dropped in rural Somerset. It is indeed a relative of Woking, and was completely rebuilt in 1938.

After seeing Templecombe's signals, our fireman is continuously at work for the next couple of miles while she roars up a long cutting, going over the top near Milborne Port at around 60mph or so. Moments later comes yet another lightning acceleration down a 1 in 80 and we are approaching Sherborne at a good 80mph. (Not so the 8.55am Ilfracombe-Waterloo, which has made a stop there and comes labouring up past us in a cloud of smoke). The romantic ruin among trees on our left is Sherborne Castle, home of Sir Walter Raleigh, the inventor of the English way of life. Can you imagine an England without chip shops or tobacconists? The station building on the up side, insofar as we are able to see it at this speed, is a particularly neat example, built from local stone. All the stations between Salisbury and Exeter were originally designed by Sir William Tite, one of the foremost architects of his day. There would appear to be two signalboxes, adjoining the level crossing. The one on the left is the original, about ready to collapse; the one on the right is being built to replace it.

By now the quantity of coal in *Clan Line's* tender has diminished to an extent where, as the fireman takes it out from the front, it is rolling and sliding down from the back and sides. A lot of dust starts swirling about, coming forward through the coal hatch, so he turns on the coal spray cock. This is simply a water supply, tapped off the rear injector output, led to a perforated pipe in the front end of the coal bunker. If it is turned full on it sprays the leading coach instead of the coal.

To reduce the amount of dust presented to the fireman, slots are cut in the shovelling plate to allow it to fall down the back of a hinged plate which forms the floor. Below that is a shelf, top of a box section joining the tender frames, on which after a few hours' running a sizeable pile of wet coal dust accumulates. If you suggested that seven years in the future someone might be crawling in there with a pickaxe to clean it out, you would presumably be joking.

Our slightly late start from Salisbury has been recovered. The driver, mentally reviewing the road ahead to Exeter, believes that delays will be unlikely, so he can ease the engine slightly, which he does. Seeing the fireman looking at him, he taps his watch and nods. His mate puts the shovel down; too thick a fire while the blast on it is light might cake up and start to cool down, which he does not want with Crewkerne bank ahead. Use of fire-irons to break it up whilst on the move is not prohibited, but it is awkward swinging a 6ft poker in a bouncing, swaying cab, and is regarded as unprofessional.

When the Salisbury & Yeovil Railway was opened in 1860 Yeovil was the obvious terminus. It was and still is by far the biggest town between Salisbury and Exeter, has grown threefold since railways reached it and is the

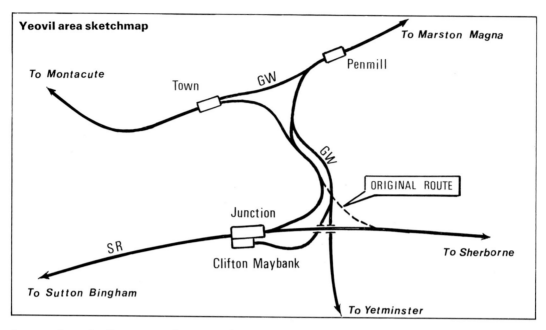

Yeovil area sketchmap

To Marston Magna

Penmill

To Montacute

Town

GW

GW

ORIGINAL ROUTE

Junction

SR

To Sherborne

Clifton Maybank

To Sutton Bingham

To Yetminster

home of such diverse products as St Ivel cheese and Westland helicopters. However, it was almost immediately bypassed by the main line and today we shall not see so much as a garden shed of it. Its main station is not only not in the town, it is not even in the same county! After crossing Wyke Gates we pass the village of Bradford Abbas, then a narrow valley, carved out by the River Yeo, winds away to the right. This leads to Yeovil. The original line turned into this valley and some of its course can still be seen, but the present line curves in the down direction to enter Yeovil Junction station. Junction to Town is served by some through trains and a local service, referred to as 'The Bunk', comprising an old LSWR push-pull set with an 'M7' class engine. As at most junctions, the branch train is not present as we go through. Nor is there anything on the line which we cross over, the ex-GWR Castle Cary-Weymouth main line, although in that case we only miss seeing another train by two or three minutes. At 1.9pm a Taunton to Weymouth train leaves Pen Mill station, 1½ miles to the north.

Yeovil Junction station dates from 1907 when it was rebuilt and enlarged with through running lines. Over to the left is a disused island platform which is in railway geography a different station, the Great Western's Clifton Maybank. It was reached by a steep curve off the Weymouth line and served solely as an interchange for goods. Also on our left, at the down end, is a turntable. No other engine

servicing facilities are visible; the shed that goes with it is two miles away at Yeovil Town.

From Yeovil Junction it is time to open *her* out again to 'full and 30' for another pull up past Sutton Bingham to a summit at Kit Hill. Then comes a real roller-coaster ride into the valley of the River Parrett at Misterton, where Crewkerne station lies, a mile from the centre of that smart market town. On the station house here, Tite's steep-pitched roofs and chimneys soar with an abandon that makes the place look about ready to take off, but a severely plain platform canopy clearly does not match it, and thereby hangs a tale of the only really alarming failure to occur on a Bulleid Pacific. On 24 April 1953, No 35020 *Bibby Line* was travelling well through the valley when her crank axle broke. Pieces of valve motion flew in all directions, demolishing the up platform canopy, but such is the safety designed into railway equipment that even in so extreme a situation the locomotive held the rails and was brought safely to a halt. Investigation established that the axle had suffered from metal fatigue, a phenomenon not understood in 1941. All the engines were immediately taken out of service and fitted with new axles in which stresses do not reach the fatigue threshold.

As we approach, the platforms cannot be seen owing to a change of gradient from 1 in 80 to 1 in 300 through the station. Beyond is an overbridge with the down starter signal standing up behind it, clearly visible from a quarter mile back. Thus reassured, the driver puts his shoulder under the regulator handle to make sure it is fully open and the fireman closes the firedoors to make sure his fire stays good and hot. He intends it to burn down a bit, as there are 13 miles of downhill to follow. A prolonged blast on the whistle is well advised; a new signalbox is being built to replace the little wooden LSWR box perched on the up platform. However, it is lunch time so no one is working on it as we rock over the points. Crewkerne goods sidings are laid out flat, so their connections have to lie at the spot where the sloping main line passes their level. Here there are a slip crossing on the up line and a three-way turnout on the down line; these are difficult structures to keep fettled up and impart a noticeable lurch to the engine.

Clan Line bores through the bridge and on up towards Crewkerne Gates, shivering the ground with her rapid-fire exhaust beats, striving to keep her speed above 60mph. It does not look as if there is a way through the high ground ahead, with Shave Hill on one side and Curriot Hill on the other, but round the next bend a Cyclopean cutting leads us to Hewish Tunnel, which is just 209yd long. It takes us through into the Valley of the River Axe, which the railway follows for 13½ miles and crosses six times.

It is around here that we should meet the up 'ACE', which is due off Sidmouth Junction at 12.50pm and past Yeovil Junction at 1.29pm. Theoretically the meeting point is about 300yd up from Hewish Gates, so that is as good a place as any to go to see the two trains. For those on board, at a closing speed of about 120mph, the passing is just a rush and a roar like any other, unless they glimpse the headboard on the other 'Merchant Navy'.

So devoid is the Axe valley of potential business that Crewkerne to Chard Junction is the longest section between stations on the entire route, eight miles. It is divided by the block post at Hewish, which has a siding at which freight is accepted, but no passenger facility, so it is not the longest block section: that distinction goes to Gillingham-Templecombe. On almost continuous down-gradients we can spin along at 80mph-plus with the engine working very economically on less than 20% cut-off and the fireman working very carefully to keep his fire bright.

Chard is a town that ought to be better known than it is by students of industrial history. Not only does it have an example of the concentration of cottage industry being incorporated into the lace factory of Gifford and Fox, it is the place where air transport was invented. William Henson and John Stringfellow saw the aeroplane as a load carrying vehicle, and drew up designs which anticipated most features of the modern airliner. They were far beyond the technology of the time, but models were built, and one tried by Stringfellow in 1848 may have been the first powered aircraft to fly. It is a sobering thought that this took place before construction of the railway had even started. Chard's railway remained a minor branch, indeed the passenger could be excused for not realising Chard Junction was a junction at all. The branch service is run by the Western Region, to find it you have to go out of the station and across the

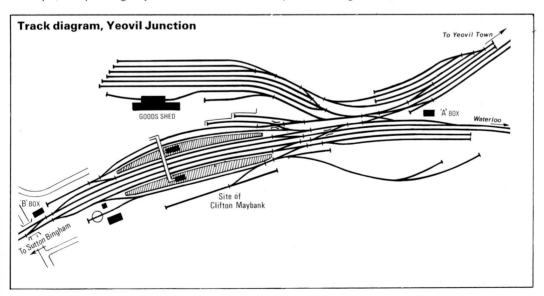

Track diagram, Yeovil Junction

To Yeovil Town

GOODS SHED

'A' BOX   Waterloo

'B' BOX

To Sutton Bingham

Site of
Clifton Maybank

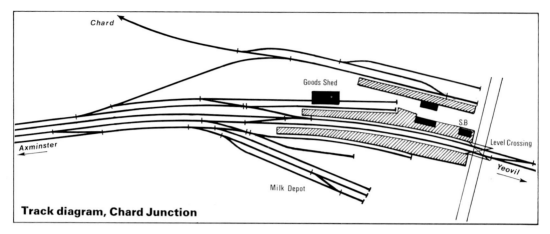

Track diagram, Chard Junction

Labels on diagram: Chard · Goods Shed · S.B · Level Crossing · Axminster · Yeovil · Milk Depot

road; these facts may or may not be connected.

The River Axe, close by on the right, forms the boundary between Dorset and Somerset. A mile and a half from Chard Junction we cross it, thus being momentarily in Dorset, and zip through Broom Gates level crossing. 200yd beyond that a stream called Blackwater River appears, to mark another boundary where we enter Devon. All these details can receive only the most cursory notice from the footplate, for the 'ACE' has covered 7⅛ miles between Hewish Crossing and Broom Gates in 5min 10-sec, at an average speed of 83mph.

It is now 1.30pm and we are approaching Axminster. This is a typical through station, with the added interest of a branch line to Lyme Regis, which starts on the north side of the main line and climbs to cross over it and head south. A third of a mile east of the station is Axminster Gates level crossing. The diagram shows the arrangement prior to 1938, in which

year it was decided that the down distant signal, positioned at Axminster Gates, was too close to the station to give adequate stopping distance. It was therefore removed and the Axminster Gates distant now protects the station. By the same argument the Axminster Gates up distant was abolished. Also in 1938, a crossover connection from the up main line to the goods sidings was removed. The track layout is far from convenient; if an up goods train wishes to do business in the yard, the locomotive must run round it via the two crossovers, draw it on to the down line and then propel it into the sidings, while to transfer

Below:
Perhaps the most famous individual engine on the route: Adams 4-4-2T No 30583 at Axminster in September 1959. On the right is a Sykes 'banner' repeater signal.
F. Tibbles

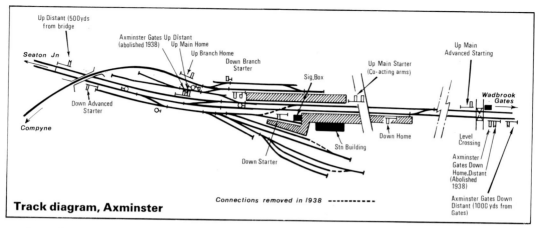

Track diagram, Axminster

Connections removed in 1938 ----------

Labels on diagram:
Up Distant (500yds from bridge)
Axminster Gates Up Distant (abolished 1938)
Up Main Home
Up Branch Home
Down Branch Starter
Up Main Advanced Starting
Seaton Jn
Sig.Box
Up Main Starter (Co-acting arms)
Wadbrook Gates
Down Advanced Starter
Compyne
Level Crossing
Down Home
Stn Building
Axminster Gates Down Home.Distant (Abolished 1938)
Down Starter
Axminster Gates Down Distant (1000 yds from Gates)

a through carriage from London into the branch requires four movements.

The first signal to greet *Clan Line* is the down distant, positioned at an overbridge on the outskirts of the town. If this is on, the driver knows he must be prepared to stop at Axminster Gates or, if the gates are clear, at the home signal or at the starter, or even at the advance starter. Only if all these four signals are off can the distant be pulled off, so the driver then knows he has a clear road through the station. However, he is not absolved from his responsibility of seeing all the other signals; an incident could occur at any time, such as a passenger falling off the platform, in which case the signalman would throw all his signals back to 'danger'. The sight of a stop signal dropping on in front of you after you had passed the distant would be the cue for an instant full brake application which could make all the difference between a close shave and a tragedy. The fact that such things happen very rarely does not affect the railwayman's constant alertness to their possibility.

The home signal marks the boundary of the previous block section, so after we have passed it another train could follow from Chard Junction, although as it happens the next one is not due for an hour. The starter gives us permission to enter the next section, but because movements to and from the goods yard must take place ahead of it, an advance starter is provided down by the branch flyover. Beyond there you definitely may not proceed without clearance from the next signalbox. Today all 'sticks' are off, indeed it would be surprising if they were not. As the 'ACE' tears through the platforms, engine exhaust inaudible beneath the mellow whistle and the multiple hammering of wheels on rail joints, the signalman sends 'train entering section' to his colleague at Seaton Junction. For us the

interest lies on the fireman's side, for in the branch line bay, just about to run round her train, is 4-4-2T No 30583.

If *Clan Line* represents the sixth generation of locomotives to work this route, the 'Adams Radials', so called because they employed the then new radial axlebox, were of the second. Designed by William Adams in 1882, they were large, fast and powerful by the standards of their day, and worked the London suburban lines until displaced by the Drummond 'M7s'. They all disappeared long ago except three, which were kept for the Lyme Regis branch because no other locomotive built since then has combined a light weight and short fixed wheelbase with sufficient haulage power for this steep, twisty little line. They are based at Exmouth Junction and work the branch on a 'one on, one off, one in the wash' basis. Maintaining three special locomotives for one branch line is an engineering headache and must be heartbreaking for the accountants, but tests are currently taking place with a LMS-type 2-6-2T No 41297 from Barnstaple depot. The enthusiast fraternity is watching the experiments closely, as the Adams Radials have been celebrities for many years because of their age and uniqueness. They have many friends, not least at Exmouth Junction depot, and the Bluebell Railway in Sussex has one on its 'shopping list', with contacts already working behind the scenes to try to ensure the preservation of an example when the time comes.

Clearly 'Lyme Billy' is not here to connect with the 'ACE', but with the 11.10am Plymouth-Brighton express which is already 'on the block' from Seaton Junction. If you wished to make the connection to Lyme you would have to travel in the last coach, which came off at Salisbury and will call here in an hour's time and meet the branch train on its next trip.

71

Above:
**Seaton Junction west end, viewed from the
branch platform on 8 May 1964. Behind the
signalbox the 8.10am Salisbury-Exeter pulls
away from the main platform, engine
No 34003 *Plymouth*. A train of tank wagons
stands in the goods yard.**
K. Stone/E. W. J. Crawforth

Below:
**The scene at Seaton Junction at about 3pm
on 17 June 1949. 'S15' No 30847 brings the
afternoon Exeter-Salisbury goods train
down the bank, while No 30455 *Sir Lancelot*
is at the platform with the 12.46 Salisbury-
Exeter (later to become the 12.36). At that
date the signals had LSWR lower-quadrant
arms.** *S. C. Nash*

There is another train standing in Axminster, occupying the up siding and effectively isolating the branch from the main line. It is a set of 40-ton hopper wagons carrying ballast from Meldon Quarry, behind a 'S15' class locomotive — the freight version of the 'King Arthur', fourth generation of West of England motive power. This train left Meldon at 10.16am and arrived here at 12.55pm, to let the up 'ACE' and the Brighton overtake it before continuing on its way.

If there is anyone on board with a stopwatch, he will not be doing anything so frivolous as looking for the number of the engine on the ballast train; he will be watching out of a left side window for mileposts, in particular milepost 146¼ which marks the end of a 13-mile descent from Hewish Tunnel. This is the fastest point in our run. *Clan Line* is in excellent general condition, less than a year after rebuilding, well-balanced on her springs, even in her action and, most importantly, free from the rattles and thumps which make fast running irksome for the enginemen. We have said that this is not a race, but the incomparable excitement of high speed on a steam locomotive has, ever since Fanny Kemble first described it in 1830, exerted its fascination on the human psyche. With a good top-link driver who knows exactly what he is doing, we can enjoy a little indulgence in its exhilaration without overstepping the bounds of safety. We can let her run. And *Clan Line* wants to run. She hurtles ahead in effortless power, seeming to come as close to flying as you are likely to get while still on the ground, purring at the chimney in ¾-regulator and 17% cut-off, casting the countryside into a mere flickering background to the two constant lines of steel which guide her. On the last couple of miles down through Axminster the speedometer needle shows 90mph, so for official purposes we will just say that we are well up to line limit.

Having crossed the Axe for the last time, we start climbing away from it on a gradient of 1 in 100 past Whitford, swinging right to cut through a spur of hill which separates the Axe from the Umborne Brook. The next station is Seaton Junction, in a beautiful setting surrounded by three hills with, on its south side, an exit to the sea down which the Seaton branch runs.

The station was originally a modest establishment similar to Sidmouth Junction which we shall see shortly, but in 1928 it was completely reconstructed. It now boasts long platforms with through lines between, extensive sidings for the milk depot and more sidings on the down side where engines off

through Seaton trains may be seen on summer Saturdays awaiting paths forward to Exmouth Junction for servicing. The branch platform curves sharply away behind the down side buildings. It is unoccupied, as the branch train is at this moment getting ready to leave Seaton in order to meet the 1.10pm stopper Exeter-Salisbury. Prominent features here are extremely tall signals on the up platform loop. The view through the station for drivers of up trains is obscured by a curve and two footbridges, so the starter signals are elevated until they can be seen from a distance above the skyline. For the benefit of drivers stopped under them, a duplicate set of arms, termed co-acting arms, is mounted lower down on the same post. The Sidmouth Junction down starter is similar.

Honiton Bank, although no steeper than some pitches we have climbed already, is more severe by virtue of its length: seven miles, most at 1 in 80, to a summit inside the west end of a 1,353yd tunnel under Honiton Hill. There is no question of rushing this bank by momentum, and it is a tribute to the quality of the motive power supplied for the line by successive designers that there is no provision for assisting engines. As *Clan Line* bursts through the road bridge at Seaton Junction at 84mph the driver begins to turn the reverser handle forward, one click at a time on its locking device. Her exhaust booms louder and louder in the firebox until it can be heard coming off the chimney in a harsh chatter, sounding more distinct as speed falls.

The fireman fires his last few rounds of the trip, swinging the black diamonds down to the front of the grate with renewed vigour although he has been at it for over an hour. Even in this modern age there are some who literally live by the sweat of their brow and we can now see it, but it does not run very far down that brow before it is dried off by the searing glare from the firehole. In order to prevent himself being grilled alive he fires eight or 10 shovelfuls at a time and then shuts the doors for a few seconds, while he checks the boiler water level and looks out at the exhaust to make sure he is not giving the engine more than she can chew. She is developing over 2,800 indicated horsepower (ihp) and still has something in reserve. Cut-off is now 38%, which the driver considers adequate to take her over the top. Past Hangman's Corner and we are down to 70mph; under the main road at Blacksands Bridge, on the steepest part of the bank, down to 60mph. The line crosses the Umborne Brook on a left-hand curve and ahead, in a delightful

Left:
Saturday 5 September 1964 was the last day of the Saturday West of England service. E. Crawforth was at the east end of Honiton Tunnel to see No 35022 *Holland-America Line* with the 11.00 Ilfracombe and Torrington . . .

Below left:
. . . and S. C. Nash was at the west end to catch No 34089 *602 Squadron* with the 10.35 Padstow and Bude.

Lower left:
The west end of Honiton Tunnel, seen from the footplate of No 34078 *222 Squadron* on 22 August 1963.
E. W. J. Crawforth

Bottom left:
On the run down from Honiton Hill, No 34010 *Sidmouth* crosses over the road three-quarters of a mile from Honiton station on 23 July 1959.
E. W. J. Crawforth

hillside setting, is the diminutive Honiton Incline signalbox. The fireman exchanges greetings with its signalman. He may be finding it a bit hot, but the engine has the job well in hand; speed is stabilising at about 50mph, boiler pressure is 220lb/sq in and with full open regulator the steam-chest pressure is 208lb/sq in. The wooded valley sides are closing in. In fact, we are in an artificial cutting, whose slopes with a century of tree growth on them merge indistinguishably with the natural contours. Round a slight right-hand curve, a black tunnel mouth appears for a few seconds before *Clan Line* charges into it. The exhaust steam now has nowhere else to go so it comes to join us in the cab, enveloping the crew in a cloud turned orange by the merciless firelight. Outside in the darkness the train of whip-cracks from the chimney hammers at the tunnel roof in a succession of shock waves felt rather than heard. The crew work calmly in the midst of this inferno, the driver holding the regulator handle in case she should slip. His mate adjusts the injector. Honiton Tunnel is perpetually wet; the chalky soil which grows splendid beech trees up above allows moisture to percolate down here to worry away at the defences of this unnatural hole in the ground, requiring constant vigilance from civil engineering maintenance staff. As she brings the train on to the easier 1 in 132 gradient in the tunnel the engine begins to speed up; after about 45sec the driver begins easing her, and as it gets light again he almost shuts the regulator. He sets the reverser to its coasting position at 45%, marked by a 'D' on the scale (it is neither necessary nor desirable to put a Bulleid into full gear when coasting, as large steam passages and 11in diameter piston valves enable her to run freely at any cut-off). Speed increases from 45mph to 60mph on a long curve from the tunnel mouth to the town of Honiton lying below the hill in the valley of the River Otter. It is the largest town in these parts, a focal point for rural industries, and receives four extra passenger trains and three

goods workings coming out from Exeter each day. The 'ACE' does not stop here, however, but hustles on through with whistle open and just a breath of steam on to cushion the moving parts of the engine. Both men find something to hold on to, as there is a diamond crossing in the down line which gives her a violent kick as she goes over it.

The injector goes full on when we leave the tunnel, to pull up the water level, which as a result of a reversal of gradient and closing the regulator, has dropped to a quarter of a glass, and to hold down the boiler pressure which has risen quickly to the red line. She does not blow-off — that is boiler control. The fireman puts the doors half shut and adjusts the blower so that it is just clearing the smoke. The fire should not need any further attention apart from levelling down with the pricker until she arrives on shed, although the fireman stays alert to its condition in case it should start to go down unexpectedly; things can happen fast on a big engine at speed. *Clan Line* cruises happily on down the hill as far as Fenny Bridges, where the line crosses the river and changes from 1 in 100 down to 1 in 100 up. A few seconds later the driver makes a partial brake application and Sidmouth Junction comes into view.

In the distance a massive eruption of smoke and steam denotes an approaching train whose engine is working hard. It is the 1.25pm Exmouth Junction-Salisbury goods, a mixed load of anything up to 500 tons, its 'S15' class engine pounding along as she has been doing any time these past 30 years and looks able to go on doing for ever. It clangs, squeaks and clatters its way through the little station as its sleek sister eases slowly in the other way in readiness to detach the Exmouth and Sidmouth coaches.

Sidmouth Junction is situated, like Seaton Junction, in the midst of a peaceful countryside. In this case the nearest village is Feniton, three quarters of a mile away, with the small town of Ottery St Mary three miles distant. There is the usual railway-based settlement

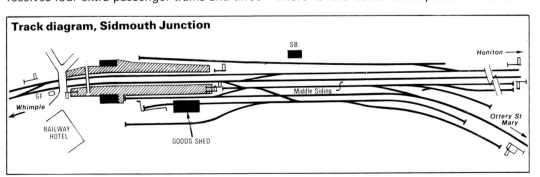

Track diagram, Sidmouth Junction

SB

Honiton →

Middle Siding

GF

Whimple

RAILWAY HOTEL

GOODS SHED

Ottery St Mary

nearby, centred on the Railway Hotel. During the 1870s one Thomas Mazely who was Rector at Plymtree, a village five miles away, would come and spend a morning each week in the hotel parlour writing an article for *The Times*, despatching it to London by train.

Some 4min are allowed to detach the Exmouth and Sidmouth coaches, which is sufficient if all is well but can be exceeded in bad weather or if couplings and hoses jam. First the train has to be stopped in the right place, with its rear end clear of the branch line connection. Since the station platform is only 480ft long and the 'ACE' is 740ft long excluding engine, only the rear seven coaches are in the platform, the rest being away beyond the starting signal, and standing over the level crossing. The station's leading porter stands on the crossing, waving the train on with a green flag and stopping it with a red one. The branch train, which arrived at 1.12pm, is meanwhile waiting beyond the platforms on the Middle Siding which makes the connection between main line and branch, its fireman taking the opportunity to have his lunch.

As we run in, our guard walks through and locks the intermediate doors where the division will be, then he alights at the end. A shunter is waiting on the platform to pluck the tail lamp from its perch. When he is satisfied that the train is stationary he drops down the narrow space between platform edge and buffers and, crouching beneath the couplings, parts the vacuum hoses. The coaches are coupled by their buckeyes, which leave little space below them. The operation of a buckeye is like a pair of hands with the fingers curled over to grasp each other. The fingers cannot open out because they are connected to a lever which projects from the palm of the coupling when they open. The knuckle of the other coupling is pressed against the palm, so the lever cannot move and the couplings both stay locked shut. To uncouple, the shunter replaces the vacuum hose on the front vehicle, but leaves the hose on the rear one off so that its brakes are held full on. He regains the platform and pulls a chain which releases the coupling lever. He does not do this until the train is ready to depart, as the chain has to be held out while the couplings are drawn apart. At this stage it may occur that the chain does not give, probably because the couplings are under tension. In that case the driver, looking back from 210yd away, must be signalled to ease up in order to free it. This done, the guard gives the right-away and rejoins the train as it draws away.

Back in the station, the shunter replaces the vacuum hose and walks to the other end of the two coaches, where the branch train is approaching under the eye of the signalman in

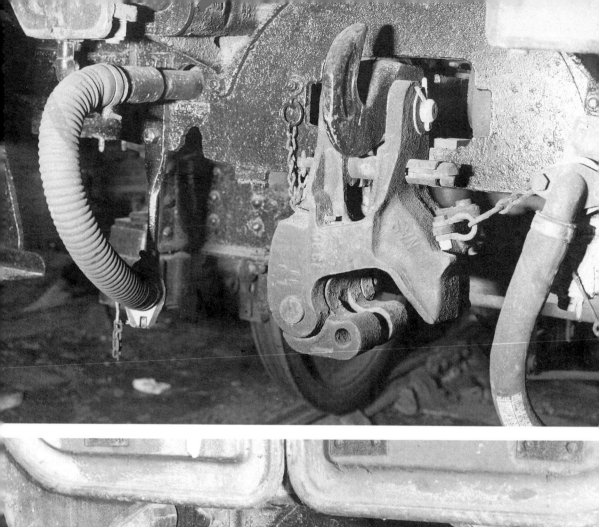
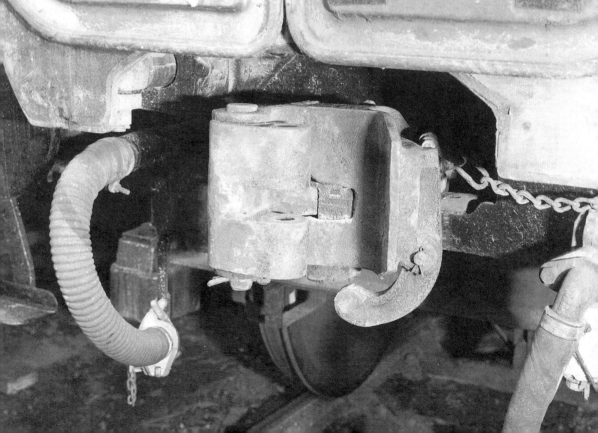

Left:
To uncouple, the chain is pulled. It operates a lever which is pushing upwards on a slide piece inside the coupling body. When that moves up, it will release the coupling fingers so that they can pivot outwards about their left-hand edge. (In actual practice this view would be obscured by the adjoining coach.)
C. Austin

Below left:
When changing from buckeye to screw coupling the buffer heads are pulled out and their shanks extended by use of collars, one of which is stowed on the right. *C. Austin*

his tall box across the line. Knowledgeable passengers in these two coaches refrain from drinking their after-lunch coffee during the manoeuvre, as the coaches have to be brought together quite positively to make the buckeye fingers spring shut. Because the buckeye is rigid it takes buffing as well as drawing loads, so the side buffers on the coach are not needed and are set back so they do not touch.

The branch train is due away at 1.52pm for a 10min run to Tipton St Johns where it leaves the Exmouth coach behind. The latter is picked

Above left:
A buckeye coupling in the dropped position ready for attachment of a screw coupling. This one was fitted on a BR Standard coach, whose drawgear is similar to the Southern standard; photographed on the Bluebell Railway in 1988. *C. Austin*

Left:
The same coupling in the operational position. To the left is the vacuum pipe on its dummy coupling, showing how the ears of the end fittings interlock. At the top is the lower edge of a detachable cover which fits on the gangway end to protect the interior sliding door from the elements. *C. Austin*

up by another train, headed by a Class 2MT (LMS type) 2-6-2T or a BR Class 3MT, to complete its journey.

The 'ACE' is due off at 1.51pm (1.49pm in the public timetable). On this occasion, thanks to our early arrival and smart station work, we are ready in good time, perhaps a shade before time. This is advantageous, for the schedule to Exeter is very tight: just 11min to Exmouth Junction, 11 miles away, albeit downhill. However, *Clan Line* is in good form for the sprint, with her safety valves once more beginning to feather. The driver takes her away and opens quickly out to full regulator and 30%. On a down gradient of 1 in 100 the acceleration is amazing. The sharp cracks from her chimney work their tempo up with every turn until they merge into a soft rippling roar. Across the River Tale the line turns to 1 in 160 up, but with only nine coaches on *Clan Line* is quite capable of accelerating on such a gradient. At the summit in a cutting near the hamlet of Talaton she is doing 62mph. Boiler pressure has fallen to 215lb/sq in, to rise again gradually as the hard pulling ceases: 60-80lb on the steam chest and 20% cut-off are sufficient and the blast becomes so light that the fireman gives her a touch of blower to keep the fire lively. She comes round another bend

into Whimple at 70mph and proceeds to demonstrate the outstanding free-running ability of the class. Speed is soon up to 85mph and remains there for the straight run down to Broad Clyst. The fireman closes down the tender coal hatch, collects up all the stray coal from on and below the shovelling-plate, hoses down the floor and refills the bucket with hot water. The back injector has to be running to supply hot water to the hose, but it is then shut off so as to leave room in the boiler to fill her up and keep pressure down after we stop.

Whimple station is notable for two features: a fine monkey-puzzle tree in the garden and the nearby Whiteways Devonshire Cider factory. Two miles further on we go full tilt over Crannaford Gates. The next station, Broad Clyst, has a pleasantly anachronistic air about it: perhaps too close to Exeter to be regarded

Above:
The Exmouth coach serves such quiet resorts as East Budleigh, where 2-6-2T No 41309 is calling on a summer day in 1963. *E. W. J. Crawforth*

as a railhead in its own right, it has not suffered any great change since it was opened in 1860. On the up side is a Permanent Way pre-assembly depot, where lengths of track complete with sleepers are loaded on flat wagons for despatch to relaying sites. Where pointwork is to be replaced, a new unit is built on the level platform in the yard here, then dismantled for transit so that it can be installed in minimum time on site. Just as we run through the station a light engine clatters by on the up road; it is the 'M7' which spends most of the day shunting at Honiton and has been back to Exmouth Junction for engine requirements. At Pinhoe the driver shuts off steam and destroys 5in of vacuum until the brakes have a steady grip on the whole train. He relies on route knowledge and experience to make a brake application of the right strength to bring about a graduated reduction of speed to 50mph as we come into sight of Exmouth Junction.

At Exmouth Junction we see standing close to the main line on our right an engine which appears to have been designed by a committee: it has a boiler from an LBSC 'C2X' class 0-6-0, cylinders from Maunsell's three-cylinder 2-6-0s, bunker and tanks reminiscent of the South Western 'Feltham' tank engines, the whole riding on eight wheels. This is the 'Z' class, referred to locally as 'ducks' for their gait on the road. Only eight were built and all are currently based here, used for shunting in the marshalling yard and assisting trains up the St David's-Central incline. The one seen here is the yard pilot and is collecting wagons for the 2.40pm departure to Templecombe. The gradient of the main line is apparent here from the height of the sidings above us at their far end, where we dive into the 263yd-long Black Boy Road Tunnel. Emerging, still slowing down, past little St Jame's Park Halt; down to 40mph now and the driver is bringing the train under control ready to stop.

While we have been speeding through Wessex, the P&D gang at Exmouth Junction locomotive depot have been preparing two more Bulleid Pacifics. For the Plymouth/ Padstow/Bude portion, duty No 581, is 'West Country' No 34033 *Chard*. For the Ilfracombe/ Torrington part, duty No 582, is 'Battle of Britain' No 34076 *41 Squadron* ('Seek and Destroy'). Although these are described as being in different classes, there is no engineering difference between them. The original idea was that the 'Battle of Britain' class should be used on Kent and Sussex routes, but such segregation never occurred in practice and became irrelevant last year when the main lines in Kent were electrified. The resultant shake-out of redundant steam engines has increased Exmouth Junction's 'WC/BB' allocation to 34 in its fleet of 120 engines.

Preparation is generally similar to that of *Clan Line* earlier, but with some differences. The valve motion, enclosed in a casing between the frames, is not on the driver's daily oiling schedule but is a fitter's job. Checking the level of 40gal of oil in a sump in the casing and draining off any water is part of the daily examination, with an inspection inside the case at the weekly examination. Because the engine has no side gangways, oil boxes for lubricating the coupled axleguides are cosily sited in the cab, but the cylinder lubricators are below the smokebox where they will collect the maximum dirt, and filling the sandboxes calls for the unprintable section of the fireman's vocabulary. In preparing the fire, she will leave the shed with it far less spread over than we saw on *Clan Line*, for the ashpan has no dampers; the air entry is permanently open, so careful control of the fire is essential to prevent it burning up too freely before it is wanted.

Nos 34033 and 34076 leave the depot coupled together for the mile and a half run down to Exeter Central, crossing to the down line as soon as the 12.15pm Exmouth-Exeter has cleared the junction. It is difficult to find

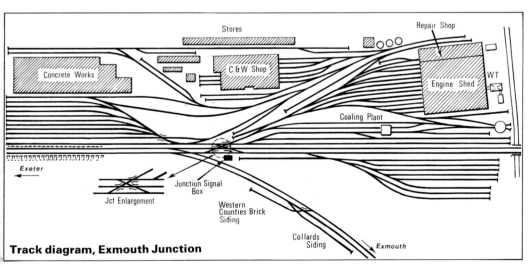

Track diagram, Exmouth Junction

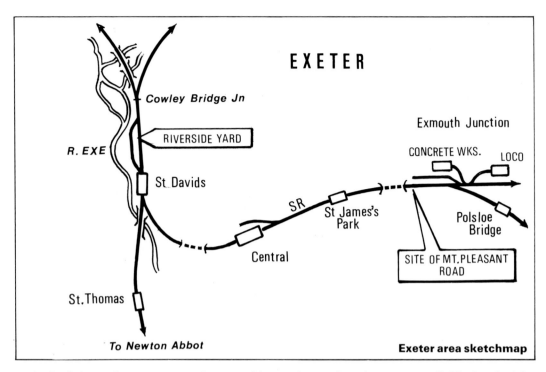

Cowley Bridge Jn

RIVERSIDE YARD

R. EXE

St. Davids

Exmouth Junction

CONCRETE WKS.   LOCO

SR

St James's
Park

Central

Polsloe
Bridge

SITE OF MT. PLEASANT
ROAD

St. Thomas

To Newton Abbot

Exeter area sketchmap

paths for light engine movements because this section is very busy: the 11.10am Plymouth-Brighton leaves at 1pm, the 9am from London arrives at 1.9pm, then we have the 1.10 to Salisbury, the 1.11pm arrival from Exmouth, the 1.15pm to Exmouth, the 11.20am ballast from Meldon leaving Central at 1.19pm, the 1.25pm to Topsham, the 1.42pm arrival from Yeovil, 1.45pm to Exmouth, 1.46pm arrival from Exmouth, 1.58pm arrival from Topsham, the down 'ACE' at 2.5pm, 2.12pm arrival from Exmouth, 2.15pm to Exmouth, 2.30pm to London, a trip goods down at 2.38pm and the 2.40pm arrival from Exmouth are the scheduled trains which make Northernhay Gardens beside the station a popular venue for enthusiasts.

The two engines run through the station on the through road into a yard at the far end used for carriage stabling. Opposite are some rail-connected warehouses, in front of which the main line dives on a gradient of 1 in 37 into a 184yd-tunnel on its way down to St David's. They move into separate sidings, and while all the lunchtime train movements are coming and going the station pilot engine finds time to shunt two coaches up to be coupled behind *Chard*. Normally there is only one, but the Central booking office advised the Train Supervisors Office this morning that they had a lot of bookings for North Cornwall and the latter, having checked with Waterloo that the

train coming down was well filled, asked for another coach. Both are corridor seconds.

Exeter Central station, called Queen Street before 1933, was built in a ravine called the Longbrook Valley, originally part of the moat of the great Norman stronghold of Rougemont Castle, which itself superseded a Roman settlement. The castle area is now a public park, although legend has it that underground tunnels survive which connect with the station drains. The original station was built rather cheaply (its roof can be seen covering the concrete plant up at Exmouth Junction), but in 1931 a complete rebuild began, with two long platforms and a splendid three-storey building at street level. The latter is in the form of a crescent 259ft long, well worth a look as it was one of the last to be built before the Southern Railway style went all curves and concrete. Although the platforms are laid out with two centre through roads, they are used for shunting movements, for nearly every train arriving here terminates or is re-formed in some way. There are carriage sidings and a small shed which is used for servicing the restaurant cars, a coal yard and general goods depot. Several transfer trips a day are needed to the marshalling yard at Exmouth Junction, where all wagons are sorted to or from Devon and Cornwall or local yards such as Newcourt on the Exmouth line, the Poltimore Brick Co on the edge of the city or the Ministry of Food

Siding, which is one of the wartime storage depots familiar throughout England. There are no massive freight hauls apart from the Meldon ballast trains, but general goods traffic supports three regular fast trains each night between here and Nine Elms. The Exmouth Junction complex includes the concrete works which since 1913 has been responsible for the uniform house style of Southern stations. It makes a range of standard items including fence panels, gates, mile and gradient posts, signal and telegraph fittings, station name-boards, lamp posts, footbridges, small buildings, loading gauges, signal posts, etc. Next door is a carriage and wagon works, opened in 1928. To make room for this the locomotive depot, opened in 1880, had to be moved further east and the site levelled by building it up. The present locomotive shed is a fine example of the use of concrete to put a big building on soft ground, using floor slabs to spread the weight. It has 13 roads, a well-equipped repair shop, an overhead coaling plant and a water tank on a high steel tower which is a landmark in the district. Exmouth Junction is, indeed, the major industrial unit in Exeter, and it is little exaggeration to say that the city, having lost its importance as a port, was in a state of stagnation until the railways arrived. The SR alone employs some 1,500 people in the town, about 5% of the working population.

At 2pm the 'M7' class engine on station pilot duty is standing on the down through road by a water column, with a shunter leaning on its cab steps, doubtless exchanging with its fireman views on the antecedents of the crew of the 'ACE'. Pilot engine crews believe they are responsible for keeping the railway running, and consider they work much harder than the old codgers on the main line who merely sit and watch the scenery go by.

As *Clan Line* comes under Howell Road bridge her driver has his brake handle in running position with the brakes almost off so that she coasts in alongside the platform at about 20mph. Then he pulls the handle down to 15in vacuum, and puts it back up. The brakes come on again, but with diminishing force as speed falls so that there is hardly a jolt as the train comes to a stop.

The driver glances at his watch. It is 2.4pm and he has gained 3min on his schedule, by running downhill slightly faster than he might normally. He drops the brake handle fully down with a whoosh of admitted air in readiness for uncoupling. The fireman is already climbing down his side of the engine. He goes to the tender, reaches in and parts the vacuum hoses. This ensures that neither the engine nor the train can move while he is between them. He unscrews the coupling and lifts it off the coach drawhook, places the tender vacuum hose on its dummy coupling, and returns to the footplate. Across the line the signalman in 'B' box, a small structure tucked almost beneath Queen Street, is watching him while he talks on the telephone to his colleague 'downstairs' at Exeter West concerning the whereabouts of the 11.46am from Plymouth which should be arriving at St Davids.

'All right, boy?' asks the driver as his fireman reappears. This seems an odd form of address to a married man with children of his own, but the fireman acknowledges it without protest; it is merely the custom of the country. *Clan Line* eases forward under the bridge on to the incline. Her next move will be back up to Exmouth Junction shed, to be turned and refuelled for her return to London with the

Track diagram, Exeter Central

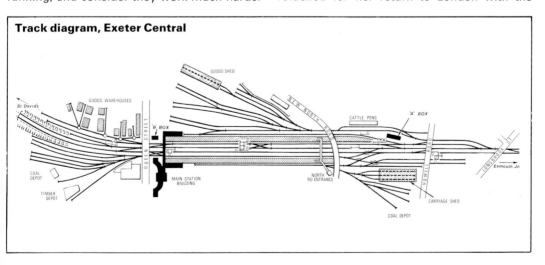

7.38pm express perishable goods train. So far today she has consumed 5 tons of coal and 7,000gal of water, figures which will be about doubled by the time she is back on Nine Elms tonight. There, another P&D crew will set about the sweltering job of breaking up and removing a couple of inches of clinker from the grate, and starting on the endless round of tasks to prepare her once more for the following day.

Boarding the footplate of *Chard*, we note some differences in the control layout. The main one is the absence of a reversing handle. The engine is equipped with a power-operated reverser, controlled by a small lever in front of the driver's seat. Cut-off is indicated by a pointer traversing a brass inscribed scale. This scale is difficult to read after a few years in situ (many senior drivers, while their long range vision remains perfect, develop the same difficulty as other mortals in reading close-to) and may have contributed to the reputation these machines have for high coal consumption, by discouraging drivers from accurately selecting short cut-offs. Two large brass oilboxes sit on the boiler backhead atop an impressive array of pipes leading to axlebox guides, etc. Another assemblage of pipework and mechanism on the backhead is the power-operated firedoor. The equipment on *Chard* looks not to have been used for some time, which is not unusual. The idea of it is that the fireman should leave the doors shut until

he is ready to fire some coal, when he pushes a pedal with his right foot and the doors open. In practice, even when it is working correctly, it is an act of some sanguinity to start a good swing with a loaded shovel in the belief that the doors will open before the shovel hits them. And some drivers, such as Fred Prickett of Nine Elms who once saw the doors close on his fireman's wrist, will not permit its use anyway. However, as one Exmouth Junction fireman said, it is just a question of getting used to it; local men do use it, and indeed it should be used because the firehole has no baffle-plate to restrict the entry of cold air. The general footplate ambience is as before: tea-can on the firehole shelf, bacon-frying sizzle in the gland of one of the Klingerflow stop valves; steady drone underfloor from the turbo-generator.

The crew who are to take her to Padstow are looking round. The driver is placing a little oil on the tender buffer shanks; smooth movement of the buffers can contribute to a comfortable ride. In standard dark green livery, *Chard's* flat casing looks rather sombre even though it is quite clean. It is not even relieved by a shield emblem, for she was never given one.

The shunter now has a busy few minutes. He has to uncouple the kitchen and dining car from the rear of the 'ACE' and couple them to the pilot engine for removal, uncouple between the fourth and fifth coaches and arrive at the front end to direct *41 Squadron* as she

Left:
The 'Ajax' patent firedoor. The steam valve, top left, is linked by a rod, running down the right of the doors, to a foot treadle.
C. Austin

Right:
The steam reverser on an original 'West Country' is controlled by one handle. It is put forward or back to select direction and rotated upwards to apply steam and move the motion. Against the cab side is a curved strip carrying the cut-off scale, over which a pointer moves. The large black handle operates the cylinder cocks. Firedoor and reverser handle were photographed on the preserved Blackmoor Vale in 1988. *C. Austin*

backs on to the Ilfracombe/Torrington portion. She departs, on time at 2.11pm, descending into the St David's tunnel.

She has just disappeared when another 'West Country' comes out with the up train from Plymouth. (The maximum load these engines are permitted to take up the incline is 200 tons, which in practice limits them to five coaches, or six at a pinch, anything heavier means taking an assisting engine. Meldon ballast trains often have two 'Zs' shoving at the rear.) Meanwhile at the east end of the down platform, the pilot engine couples up to the kitchen and diner and shunts them on to the through road. They will return to London on the 4.30pm up, providing sustenance to travellers from Padstow, Plymouth, Torrington and Ilfracombe. Left at the platform are three coaches. *Chard* backs on with her two, making

the load up to five, 174 tons tare, about 188 tons loaded. It is 17min since we arrived when our new guard gives the right away for the second portion. *Chard* moves briskly off with a few sharp exhaust beats, then coasts the length of the platform and noses over the scissors crossing with the driver already putting the brake on to steady her down into the tunnel and on to the Western Region.

Below:
Exeter Central station and goods yard, seen from New North Road. A short train is at the down platform, a pilot engine on the through road, and No 34038 *Lynton* departs with an up train leaving an assisting engine behind. (5 August 1955). *J. Robertson*

A Change of Pace

As *Chard* emerges from St David's tunnel her driver is presented with a splendid view across the Exe Valley, with the river immediately below and the suburbs of St Thomas and Exwick extending up the wooded slopes beyond. The fireman is watching the approach of St David's station on the right as the train, brakeblocks holding firmly to bring us down to 10mph, nears a lower-quadrant signal belonging to Exeter West.

Exeter St David's opened in 1844 as the terminus of the Bristol & Exeter Railway and saw its continuation in the form of the South Devon Railway. That was the line which worked for a time on the atmospheric system, one of whose pump-houses still stands, incorporated into the railway gasworks. The present station dates from a rebuilding in 1914. Because all South Western traffic has to pass through it, a truce was necessary with the Great Western, but it was a fragile thing; the GWR made it clear that the station belonged to them and exacted an agreement that all LSWR trains would stop there. While the terms on running rights were scrupulously observed, it frequently occurred that the Cowley Bridge signalman had a slow goods unaccountably delayed in section just as a South Western boat express was due. We may expect that various attempts were made to build a separate line, indeed work was actually started in 1935 to create a site for a Southern St David's, but it made little progress.

Below:
A view from Exeter St David's across Red Cow level crossing on 2 April 1950, as the up 'ACE' Padstow portion comes in behind No 34014 *Budleigh Salterton*. The crossing was not a public right of way, so the railway used to close it for one day a year, traditionally Christmas Day. The beam in the 'four-foot' is a GWR ATC ramp, to which Southern engines do not react. *B. A. Butt*

Above:
Cowley Bridge Junction on 22 September 1953, with 34017 *Ilfracombe* on an up train from Ilfracombe, joining the down GWR line. *C. F. H. Oldham*

Down SR trains run through St David's in the opposite direction to down Western trains. On the Plymouth road, those same trains pass Lydford station in the opposite direction to down trains on the Western's Launceston line, and arrive in Plymouth in the Western's up direction. Exmouth Junction men will tell you that it is the other lot who are going the wrong way. When they pull *Chard* up in Platform 4, they are faced with people and cars streaming across in front of them with no barrier. Red Cow level crossing is very busy as it serves one of only five road bridges across the River Exe below Tiverton. Crossing 14 tracks, it could claim to be the longest level crossing in the world.

Six signalboxes control the area: Exeter West, Goods Yard, Middle, Riverside, East and Cowley Bridge Junction. The last-named employs a regulator, a signalman who is authorised to control trains in a local area, as

distinct from passing them through, and to take decisions on the despatch of trains according to the ability of their destinations to receive them.

We get the tip to go, on time at 2.25. For the moment we are still an express, with an 18½ mile run to North Tawton non-stop in 28min, but the speed is markedly lower. The work required from *Chard* and her fireman is not very heavy with so light a load, although to keep time between the stops entails smart acceleration and the gradients should not be underestimated. The fireman maintains a thin bright fire over the grate, but with a mound under the door which facilitates rolling coal into the back corners.

When working short distances between stops, a different technique is used from the continuous effort we have seen so far. The engine is started away with the firedoors shut. When we are up to speed and she has been eased to a short cut-off, the appropriate quantity of coal is put on the fire. The injectors are off. The fireman completes the round in time to catch the distant signal for the next station, and when the driver shuts off he starts an injector, opens the firedoors slightly to avoid smoke and perhaps applies a touch of blower. By the time the station stop is over, the boiler is full again and the fire is burnt through ready for the next pull. As *Chard* gets going on the virtually level line past Exeter Riverside yard we appreciate some more differences from the rebuilt engines in the way she is behaving. Her valve motion is lighter and she has smaller balance weights in the wheels. There is therefore very little hammer-blow effect, giving her a very smooth action. She is light on her feet — we will not have to test her ability to start or stop a heavy load — and rides like a coach. When we look out of the front window, however, we find that half the world is blocked off by the high slab side of the casing, leaving us a narrow slit formed by the front deflector plate through which to view the road ahead. Clearly knowledge of the route is going to be even more important if we are to find the signals, without benefit of AWS. On the left side, the driver is about to commune with the steam reverser. Using this gadget is theoretically simple; you have a steam cylinder to move the reversing shaft and a hydraulic cylinder to lock it. You open a valve which bypasses the locking cylinder and then open a two-way steam valve to move the motion to the desired position. The snag is that the steam cylinder is amply powerful and the pointer zooms along its scale so enthusiastically that you might or might not stop it in the right place. Trying to link up from 25% to 20% could well result in the thing going into back gear, which when travelling forwards does not do any good. On the other hand, any failure will let it drop into full forward gear, but she can cope with that as long as there is no subsequent need to reverse. Faced with this, most drivers pull it up to a favoured position, usually around 25%, and leave it there, driving on the regulator, until the next stop when they put it into full gear for the restart.

Heading north from Exeter, we are hardly under way before easing to observe the 25mph limit over Cowley Bridge Junction. The perceptive traveller realises that we are bound for a different kind of country from the rich South Devon farmlands or the Riviera surroundings on the GWR's Tor Bay; a country harsher and more exciting. *Chard* takes the left turn, over two bridges, and sets out on an almost unbroken 26-mile climb to the foothills of Dartmoor. The legendary uncontrollable Bulleid Pacific steaming does not seem to be living up to expectations, indeed the steam is going down, even with the injectors off. The fireman has a look round the fire under his inverted shovel blade and decides that it is not quite right; it is too heavy at the back and too

thin at the front. He sets to work to correct it, pushing the nearer part down with the shovel and putting some on at the front. Getting it right, with no thin patches or thick masses, is indicated within a very few minutes by the pressure gauge rapidly swinging over towards the red line. If he overdoes it, despite the absence of ashpan dampers, the fire can always be cooled down by blacking the rear part of it out again, or even by making a hole in it. The latter does not seem to harm the fireboxes, but the better firemen regard it as unprofessional and control the boiler on a 'West Country' as on any other engine by applying the right amount of coal at the right time.

Meanwhile, outside the cab, the rich meadows that produce Devonshire cream are sliding past. The River Yeo provides a convenient route, not too steep, so the railway follows it through Newton St Cyres and Crediton, crossing over it eight times on the way. *Chard* runs easily on half regulator and 25%, making a noise which could, at the moment, be described as 'puffing'. This was originally a Broad Gauge line, with the generous clearances and good alignment of that genre and even a little Brunel-type villa station at Crediton. More important on the railway map is Yeoford, a small village tucked

Below:
Two 'West Countries' meet on the North Devon line. The approaching engine, No 34107 *Blandford Forum*, **is equipped with AWS, unlike those in many of the earlier photographs, and carries a battery box above the buffer beam.** *E. W. J. Crawforth*

away amidst narrow, winding, lanes. During the early hours of the morning four goods trains are made up here at once; shunting goes on round the clock, usually by one of the Exmouth Junction's three '700' class Drummond 0-6-0s. While the two sections of the 'ACE' go by, the 8.20am Plymouth-Exmouth Junction goods train is being remarshalled in the yard. Our approach coincides with that of the afternoon Meldon ballast train, coasting downhill behind an 'S15' 4-6-0, going rather fast for a freight train, but do not worry, its wagons are all brake-fitted. The valley gets narrower and the surrounding hills higher, the road gets steeper and slows us down to 40mph. The driver lets her carry on like this as there is a speed limit at Coleford Junction, so at 35mph she takes the left fork and at once begins climbing much more steeply up a side valley. As we gain height the scenery begins to open out and we see further and further across the top of the rolling hills. *Chard* is accelerating effortlessly up the 1 in 80, and on a short downhill stretch approaching Bow she attains 60mph. The fireman comes over to the left side to observe the signals on the left-hand bend, standing holding on to the narrow cab bulkhead behind the driver's seat, the while informing the world of his intention to visit Widecombe Fair with Uncle Tom Cobbleigh and All (fortissimo).

'He were a native of these parts, you know, Tom Cobbleigh', remarks the driver. 'He lived at Spreyton, just up the road from where we are now.'

He reaches up and gives a short toot on the whistle to remind the staff at Bow that we are not stopping. Beyond a bridge over the infant River Yeo (just to confuse you, this is not the Yeo we have been following, it is another one that flows north to join the Taw) the up-gradient resumes for a mile and a half. Now with a bit more regulator, but still on 25%, *Chard* talks rather more loudly. The fireman attends to his fire, then looks out again for North Tawton's signals. Observance of signals is entirely by sight once we are west of Exeter; *Chard* is fitted with AWS Equipment, but it remains silent, as the accompanying track magnets have not been installed on this route. Fortunately today is very clear, with that after-rain brightness, and the view to our right now stretches away to Exmoor, some 20 miles away.

North Tawton station, where we make a very brief stop, seems far too grand for its rural location. The explanation is that in pre-railway days North Tawton was the principal town of the district, bigger than Okehampton, so naturally it was given a commensurate station. Whatever hopes the local community leaders may have entertained of future prosperity, the railway had a contrary effect, as the populace used it to take their business to Okehampton and Exeter. Poor old North Tawton went into decline and never really did justice to this splendid station house with its 12 chimney stacks. By comparison, Sampford Courtenay is about the least of all the stations; it really only exists because from January 1867 to October 1871 it was the terminus. It is the smallest of the stations on the line, and has the least service, being missed out by all the through London trains, which might explain why its gardens are magnificent with a notable display of topiary. It is rather surprising, therefore, to see a Bulleid Pacific shunting out the tiny goods yard as we pass; that is the 11.15am Plymouth-Yeoford goods, which has been picking up wagons all the way round Dartmoor since we left London this morning.

The start from North Tawton is possibly the smartest on the whole run, for it is made on a 1 in 80 down. The driver does not even have to set *Chard* to a longer cut-off to get away, and on his standard 25% cut-off she is up to 40mph before reaching the Taw river bridge; 120lb/sq in on the steam-chest makes her accelerate further up the 1 in 77, but about a mile and a half past Sampford Courtney a right-hand curve appears and he eases her to conform to a 45mph speed limit which applies as far as Okehampton. The country is extremely difficult for railway-building on this length and it is remarkable that the builders managed to stick to their ruling gradient. The big overbridge is the main A30 road, from which we drop down to a solid stone viaduct over the wooded valley of the East Okement River. The line now takes up a position on the side of the valley and continues, still climbing, towards Okehampton station, set high above the greystone town.

'It was difficult to work on a West Country all day without letting her blow off' — 'Smokey'.

Okehampton is best known as the last home of the 'Greyhounds', Dugald Drummond's 'T9' class 4-4-0s. These beautiful locomotives were built in 1899-1900, displacing the elegant Adams 4-4-0s on top-rank express services until they were in turn displaced by more powerful locomotives only five years later as train weights and speeds increased. Of the original 66, 14 remain, eight of them based on Exmouth Junction whence they work local

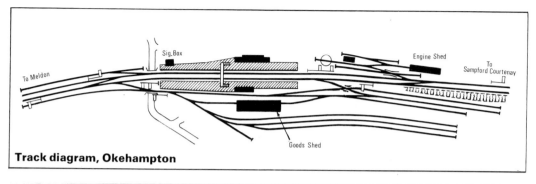

Track diagram, Okehampton

traffic to Plymouth and Cornwall. They are probably the finest engines to run on the LSWR and only now, with numbers of modern machines becoming redundant in Kent, are they reaching the end of their road.

The station is built on a ledge on the moor side at an altitude of 750ft above sea level, with a single-road engine shed on the edge where there seems very little reason why it should not plunge into the East Okement River 120ft below. The present arrangements date from early Southern Railway years with the exception of the turntable. A 70ft table was built in 1947 to permit large engines, up to the new 'Merchant Navies', to turn when working Meldon ballast trains. Trains are joined and divided here, no small task given the restricted track layout. The first portion of an up train has to draw right out of the station while the second portion is brought in and its engine removed, the operation taking some 20min. At least the passengers have a splendid view over the town towards Abbeyford Woods, or up the slopes of Dartmoor.

Above:
A Padstow train in the down loop platform at Okehampton: 'Greyhound' (Drummond 'T9' class) No 30718 and two-coach set No 28. It is thought to be the 12.58pm departure, some time in 1960-61.
E. W. J. Crawforth

The engine to take on the Plymouth coach is standing in the loop platform; probably another 'West Country', but it could be a 2-6-0 or a 'T9'. A corridor brake second is attached to it, with some passengers already aboard — it is warm today but not too warm — and it will set back on to the through coach when we have left the latter behind. Detaching is the same as we saw earlier at Sidmouth Junction. There are also parcels and mails to be loaded and unloaded, for although the 'ACE' is just one of many expresses leaving London, down here its arrival is the main railway event of the day. In any event, there is no point in moving off until the 12.58pm from Padstow is belled on from

Meldon Junction because the railway beyond that point is single track and we would have to wait until it is clear. The Plymouth portion is not going on to a single track but will still have to wait in order to provide a connection from the Padstow. Meanwhile, to complicate matters the 2.25pm from Plymouth should now be between Lydford and Bridestowe on its way up. If it were late, it would delay us because at Meldon Junction we have to turn right, which we cannot do until it has passed. It is due there at 3.20pm and we are timed at 3.22pm.

Our schedule allows 2hr 7min from Okehampton to Padstow. Since it is 62¼ miles by rail and only 53 by road, this does not seem very fast to the new generation of travellers weaned on the freedom of the open road. They do not, of course, imagine that the motorist of a quarter-century later, queuing for 2hr in summer just to get across the Camel bridge at Wadebridge, would regard a conveyance that went through from Okehampton to Padstow in that time as a miracle.

Okehampton stationmaster is out on the platform overseeing operations. As the down signals are 'on', he orders the uncoupling to take place, so *Chard's* driver draws forward a few feet and stops again. The fireman puts some water in, to keep her quiet and also ensure that she has a full glass when she cocks her tail up over the summit. He looks out to exchange waves with his colleague on the up Padstow as it comes in past him at 3.13pm. At 3.14pm the signals come off. We whistle up, get a green flag from the guard and at 3.15pm we are off, *Chard* making light of the climb now that her four-coach train is lighter than she is.

Two miles further on and 140ft higher is the great gash in the hillside that is Meldon Quarry. We can tell we are nearing it by the greyness imparted to the landscape by dust

from blasting, before we come up alongside a huge flat area occupied by crushing and grading plant, sidings and loading bunkers, beyond which lies the workface where Black Down is being steadily gouged away at a rate of over 300,000 tons a year. The stone is not the granite with which Dartmoor is normally associated, but a hard limestone, ideal for railway ballast. There is nothing beautiful about Meldon — even the signalbox is a plain block resembling a wartime pillbox — and country-lovers would prefer to see it closed down. However, local people see it differently; anything that offers employment in North Devon is ipso facto a thing of beauty.

Meldon has its own shunting engine, housed in a primitive shed. At present the engine is 'O2' class 0-4-4T No 30199. An elderly passenger tank engine is clearly unsuited to shifting massive bogie hopper wagons around, but she is only a stand-in since the previous incumbent, 'G6' 0-6-0T No 30272 (known to her

Below left:
The driver on No 34036 *Westward Ho* is supposed to be able to see where he is going, and to see the Okehampton up starter as he starts away past an engine in the shed yard on 28 December 1962. Also, someone will have to clear the snow from point rods and signal wires.
E. W. J. Crawforth

Below:
Another impression of Dartmoor's winter face as No 34110 *66 Squadron* comes out of a blizzard on 27 February 1962 and passes Meldon Quarry. The foreground is the tender of 'N' No 31843, with fire-irons lying on the coal with their ring handles hooked over stout posts. E. W. J. Crawforth

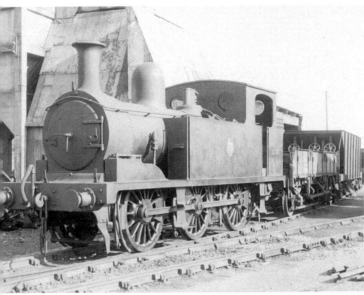

Left:
The Meldon Quarry shunter, 'G6' No DS682, at work in 1961. The '02' was basically the same design with a 0-4-4 wheel layout. The second wagon is one of the special 40-ton bottom door ballast wagons.
E. W. J. Crawforth

Below left:
Fireman's view of Meldon Viaduct from a 'T9'. Ahead, next to a crane parked on the Quarry shunting neck, is a signal post bearing the Quarry advance starter, Meldon Junction distant, Quarry entrance backing arm, and a 20mph speed limit sign.
E. W. J. Crawforth

Bottom:
Meldon Viaduct: north side, looking towards the quarry. The engine on top is *Chard*, hauling a Plymouth train on 1 May 1952. *M. E. Ware*

friends as DS3152) was withdrawn on or about 9 August. A replacement 'G6', No 30238 latterly of Guildford, has been allocated the job but will not be ready for another month or so.

At the far end of the quarry lies Meldon Viaduct. The structure comprises six spans, each 86½ft long, with a maximum height of 113ft above ground, built entirely of steel on low stone plinths. The setting is incomparable: the West Okement River runs beneath in a deep ravine, to our right is farmland sloping up to Maddaford Moor and to the left, only 1¾ miles away, the peak of Yes Tor, highest of the Dartmoor Tors at 2,028ft, stands hard below scudding clouds.

As we pass the quarry reservoir *Chard's* driver eases the regulator back and carefully adjusts the reverser to 30%. She slows to 20mph over the viaduct, then he gives her more steam to keep moving on the gradient which steepens to 1 in 58 through a cutting, at the far end of which Meldon Junction comes into view. The signals are still at danger. The fireman sits down on his seat.

The 'West Country'-hauled Plymouth train accelerates past (the signalman held it until he saw us coming because only one train is allowed on the viaduct at a time); its coaches are bound for Waterloo where they will arrive combined with Padstow, Ilfracombe and Torrington coaches, at 8.0pm. The right-hand junction signal goes up. At 10mph *Chard* noses right over the points. The fireman comes over to the left side and leans over the side door to receive from the signalman a large metal hoop carrying a strong leather pouch in which is a single-line tablet for the section Meldon Junction-Ashbury. It is hung on one of the steam valves over the boiler backhead. *Chard* throws up her cloud of exhaust, looking insignificant in this wide landscape, drops down to the main road and gallops up the other side towards Thorndon Down, past Maddaford Moor Halt which is the last

Above left:
At Meldon Junction the branch to Halwill curves away across the background. The up Padstow/Bude 'ACE' is seen coasting down towards the viaduct, shortly before 11am on 9 May 1961; the locomotive is No 34110 *66 Squadron*. S. C. Nash

Left:
No 34081 *92 Squadron* near Maddaford Moor halt on 11 May 1961, hauling two corridor seconds and the Padstow and Bude coaches. S. C. Nash

platform we shall pass without stopping. The next station, Ashbury & North Lew, is essentially a passing place, North Lew being a village about 2½ miles away, although it is useful to farmers as a distribution centre for incoming fertilisers and foodstuffs, and outgoing produce and livestock. Indeed, goods storage in three substantial sheds far exceeds passenger accommodation in a small single-storey building. The signalman here, having cleared the road, steps across from his box on the up platform carrying an Ashbury-Halwill tablet, which he exchanges for the other one. Both driver and fireman glance at the tablet to make sure that it does in fact have 'ASHBURY TO HALWILL' stamped on it, as every engine crew has done since a day 40 years ago when a driver who omitted this precaution set out on his last journey from the Welsh station of Abermule. The tablet-change routine is carried out at every stop from now on. Tablet changing should be done at 10mph, but if the crew are in a hurry, higher speeds are not unknown.

The railway runs along Broadbury Down, never straight and level anywhere but gradually descending to Halwill Junction or, as it proudly describes itself, 'Halwill for Beaworthy, Junction for Bude, North Cornwall and Torrington Lines'. The country hereabouts is pretty bleak and empty outside the holiday season, the railway settlement called Halwill Junction is the largest village for miles around, so it is not surprising that the passenger station is another modest bungalow, but it is surrounded by a big goods yard with two warehouses, a sorting yard, massive signal gantries and a lofty signalbox. Opposite where we come to rest, as an afterthought tacked on to the up platform, a short bay line is the grand terminus of the North Devon & Cornwall Junction Railway (ND&CJR), whose one-coach passenger trains meander their way to Torrington twice a day. Since its opening in 1925, as a Government-sponsored project to improve this impoverished district, the ND&CJR has pursued its secluded life, untroubled by such vulgar considerations as the profit motive, apart from an embarrassing moment in 1951 when it obtruded itself on the public consciousness by staging a collision between a train carrying a driver, fireman, guard and one passenger and a bus carrying a driver, conductor and no passengers. If you wish to patronise it you should take the Torrington coach of the 'ACE' which connects with the 4.0pm Torrington-Halwill. That is not exactly a fast train, taking 1hr 20min to cover 20 miles, but one cannot deny that hamlets like

Below:
On 12 May 1961, *66 Squadron* had only one Exeter-Padstow coach to go with the Padstow and Bude coaches, but this time Exmouth Junction depot had found a headboard. S. C. Nash

Meeth and Petrockstowe have a service to London with only one change.

At Halwill, as at Okehampton, a shunter uncouples our last coach, which is to be taken forward to Bude by a 2-6-2T standing in the down-side bay with a two-coach set, a brake second and a brake composite. The 4min station stop is slightly extended by a need to off-load some packages and for the driver to visit the station amenities — he has been on the road for 2hr and there is of course no provision on a steam locomotive. As the 'ACE' accelerates away round the sharp left-hand curve from the junction the driver gives a sudden exclamation. A pheasant appears flying across from our left towards Halwill Moor Plantation and looks to be on a collision course. Unfortunately the fireman is checking the state of the fire and looks out rather too late.

Any bird which trespasses on the railway and meets a train is regarded as fair game, but the small front platform on a 'West Country' is poor for collecting the victim in comparison

with, say, a 2-6-0, so if we did hit it the likelihood is that it will have bounced off. In that case the lengthman will probably pick it up on his inspection walk of the track.

Halwill is situated on top of one of the most exposed parts of Devon, a watershed whence streams flow northwards to form the River Torridge to reach the sea at Appledore, or southwards to join the Tamar. The North Cornwall line takes the south route, following the River Carey all the way to Launceston; a 14-mile descent from 650ft altitude to 200ft at Polson Bridge, on a ruling gradient of 1 in 73. The work for *Chard* is therefore very easy except for the start away from Tower Hill where the line rises slightly to effect a river crossing, and a climb at 1 in 94 from Polson Bridge into Launceston.

Ashwater station is in a particularly lovely setting at a hamlet called Ashmill, in a narrow valley so secluded that the only roads to penetrate it are steep, narrow lanes. On arrival the fireman hurries round to the front of the engine, but there is no sign of that pheasant. Except when firing, he travels mostly sitting by his open window, for it is a sunny afternoon and the cab interior is rather warm. The driver opens her up a bit over the next section to make up some time: not that folk indulge in that ridiculous London habit of clock-watching, but it is desirable to be punctual at Launceston because we pick up a number of school-children. At Tower Hill, a more open site lower down the valley, the stationmaster meets us to exchange pleasantries.

After another fast run we come to where our valley emerges into the broader Tamar, which we are going to cross, and continue into another side valley opposite. From a long embankment the river comes into sight with a farm on the bank and the main A30 road in the woods to the left — Polson Bridge and at 4pm we are entering Cornwall. The GWR line from Plymouth comes up the Tamar from the left, at a lower level on the opposite bank of a smaller river, the Kensey. Ahead through *Chard's* narrow windows, Launceston town extends up a hillside to the round tower of its Norman castle. Its title of 'Gateway to Cornwall' is apt, because the boundary of Cornwall is a real one. Below Polson only three roads and two railway lines cross the Tamar. The GWR line crosses beneath ours and runs into a terminus, but since 1952 its trains have used the former LSWR station via a connection in the approaches. The link was one of many put in during World War 2 to improve the flexibility of the railway network; before then the two companies would have scarcely acknowledged each other's existence.

Below:
On 30 April 1964 2-6-2T No 41214 with a 'loose' (not allocated to a set) BCK stands in the NDCJR bay at Halwill ready for the evening trip to Torrington at 6.30. The station proper is to the right. M. York

North Cornwall

As we run into Launceston (pronounced Larnson) the 11.35am Wadebridge-Okehampton goods train is shunting in the yard. The engine of this is a Class N 2-6-0, which may be reckoned as the fifth generation of South Western motive power since, although it is a contemporary of the King Arthur we saw earlier, it is a more advanced design. It originated on the South Eastern & Chatham Railways, whose Chief Mechanical Engineer, REL Maunsell (pronounced Man-Sell) came from Swindon drawing office and went on to hold the post on the Southern Railway until 1937. His 2-6-0s included many features developed at Swindon during the early years of this century, such as a high-pressure boiler with tapered barrel, long-travel piston valves, mechanical vacuum pump and smokebox regulator. The 'Ns' are

excellent general purpose engines capable of working any train almost anywhere. The goods train is obviously not ready to leave although it should go as soon as we have passed. Further indication that something is wrong is the presence on the platform of the stationmaster and another man who has on his left arm a red band bearing the word 'Pilotman'.

The electric tablet system is vital to the operation of these lines which are single track. Where trains in both directions have to use the same track there must clearly be rigid measures to preclude two trains meeting. This is regarded as so important that whenever a single-line railway was opened the company had to deliver to the Government a legal oath, over its common seal, that only one engine in steam would ever be permitted to enter a

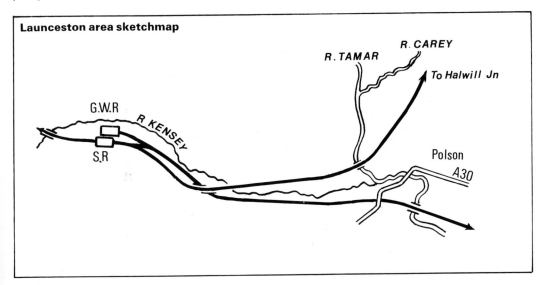

Launceston area sketchmap

R. CAREY

R. TAMAR

To Halwill Jn

G.W.R

R KENSEY

S.R

Polson

A30

single line section at one time. To enforce this, besides the control of the signalling system, the driver must carry a unique, tangible device authorising him to enter the section. In this case that is the tablet, which is a metal plate with a slot cut in it so that it engages in a rack in the electric tablet instrument. There are two identical instruments in the signalboxes at each end of the section, each containing several tablets, and they are electrically locked and connected so that when a tablet is withdrawn from either instrument, both are locked and will not release another tablet until the first one has been replaced in either instrument. If any breakdown occurs in the equipment, the signalmen will, even if they know the section is clear, treat it as blocked and will stop the traffic rather than violate the integrity of the tablet system. To get things moving a man is appointed to take the place of the tablet: he is the pilotman.

What happened today was that at about 2.30pm the Egloskerry signalman found he could not withdraw a tablet to allow the goods train to proceed to Launceston. He therefore telephoned his colleague and between them they agreed that there was nothing in the section and the system had failed. The Launceston stationmaster then appointed a pilotman (who happens to be the lengthman) and gave him the requisite Pilot Working Forms. The latter went to Egloskerry on his motorbike — it is only five miles by road — issued a form to the signalman there and accompanied the train back to Launceston. Next, he rode down on the 9.30am Yeoford-Wadebridge goods, collected his bike and rode it back to be ready for the 'ACE'. Meanwhile, a lineman has been called to investigate the fault. As soon as he has cleared it the pilotman will visit both signalboxes to collect and cancel his Pilot Working Forms, tablet working will be resumed, and the problem will be solved without the travelling public being aware of it. All of this may seem to the layman to be a bit of a pantomime; but even nowadays, reports of disasters in other countries where procedures are less strict show that these precautions are conducive to the safety which we take for granted when we travel by train.

Our disabled passenger is being assisted from the train by the stationmaster in person — this is nothing like Waterloo. The pilotman has to obtain permission from the signalman to proceed, and disappears over to the up platform where the box is situated. 'We'll put the pipe in while we're waiting', says the driver. No water stop is booked for the 'ACE' between Exeter and Padstow, but if the opportunity arises enginemen will usually prefer to take on more water should they be stopped at a column: the more water you have the less will be your concern about when you can get more. A steam engine without water in its tank is just a lump of metal. *Chard* is watered, then the pilotman returns and we are off, feeling vaguely offside about passing the starter signal at danger.

The lightly loaded engine chatters her way into speed on another 1 in 77 out of Launceston. The outstanding characteristic of the North Cornwall line is that nowhere is it straight or level, and very little of it is not in a cutting or on an embankment. It only has four passenger trains each way per day during the winter, none on Sundays, giving the signalman at Egloskerry just over 11hr in which to deal with a traffic that would occupy Clapham Junction for about 4¼min. However, two of those trains go through to or from London: the 'ACE' and the newspaper train which leaves Waterloo at 1.15am. There are also two goods trains each way. On a summer Saturday the number of passenger trains each way increases to 13, not counting reliefs. The stations are all built to the same design, using local stone except at Egloskerry and Tresmeer where the houses are in brick. The names, too, are part of the Cornish atmosphere. We note 'Eglos' resembling 'Eglwys' or 'Eglise' (anglice Church) and recalling the lost Cornish language. Tresmeer is undoubtedly more euphonious than the actual name of the village containing the station, which is Splatt. Camelford: 'Camel' means 'crooked river'. Railway publicity draws a connection to Camelot and convinces you that King Arthur did everything but catch a train there, and a Southern National Omnibus connects with the 'ACE' for romantic Tintagel and Boscastle. Padstow is a contraction of Petrockstowe, a chapel founded by St Petroc.

At Egloskerry, where the pilotman gets off, the stationmaster and porter-signalman have just finished checking the contents of some wagons left by the up goods train — the only one that stops here, down traffic has to be staged through Wadebridge — and are assembling a pile of crates on the up platform. They are for the 3.13pm Padstow-Exeter, which conveys at least two braked and heated vans for parcels traffic. The latter is mostly perishable produce, hence the local name for the train of 'The Perisher'. Although the hard days when large numbers of Cornwall's inhabitants emigrated on the railway are over, there are still plenty of one-way tickets issued at these little stations — mostly for rabbits by the grateful.

Chard is urged with some vigour up the Kensey valley, causing the fireman to fire an extra round, reaching nearly 60mph which feels very fast indeed on this twisty road. In spite of this, the 3.13pm, with a 'T9' on the front, is already in Tresmeer station. The road is set and the signals off, so our stop is barely longer than it takes to exchange tablets. Off again, still climbing through a country that gets higher and wider as we go. There is a valley between Treneglos and Scarsick which we cross on an embankment 86ft high. Trees become smaller, hugging eastern slopes and gullies between great sweeps of downland occupied only by sheep. Otterham station is in a magnificent setting nearly 800ft above sea level. There is nothing like a village in sight, but several people are waiting for the train, and in the little goods yard a hayrake is being off-loaded from a wagon while some men are transferring sacks of something agricultural on to weatherbeaten Land Rovers. Among the alighting passengers are heard American voices. During the war an airfield, which still

exists, was built a couple of miles away on Davidstowe Moor, the only sizeable area hereabouts that is anything like flat. At 970ft it is the highest airfield in Britain and must be a strong contender for the title of the bleakest. American Army Air Force boys must have been horrified to find themselves dumped here in an English winter, but the Cornish magic went to work on them and now, 16 years later, they are bringing their families to experience it. When they leave the station entrance they will see what those on the train see when it has pulled out past the road bridge: to the right, northwest, a sector of the horizon is a level blue line. Take a good look, for notwithstanding the board fitted to the smokebox of our engine, that is the first and on this run the only sight of the Atlantic Ocean.

It is as the 'ACE' forges up the last mile to Otterham summit that we appreciate the comfort of a 'West Country's' enclosed cab. This is a fine, sunny afternoon, but a constant blast of wind is sweeping across the country, snatching away *Chard's* exhaust before we have a chance to see whether it is light grey or any other colour. No wonder the few trees are all wedge-shaped, angled from right to left. To a city-dweller, the sheer quantity of air up here can only be described as breath-taking. A passenger on the footplate might well be thinking at this moment that to be able to earn your living by travelling this scenery must be an idyllic life. Of course, it doesn't look quite

the same in winter with sleet coming in one cab doorway and straight out the other, and if he were shunting at Otterham yard on a winter evening, in the open-backed cab of a 2-6-0 or 'T9', he might take a different view of it.

The fireman makes a mound of coal at the back of his fire, checks the bounce of the water in the gauge-glass as he twists its drain-cock, adjusts the injector water key, draws over his cab side windows and pours out a cup of tea.

For the next mile the unending sequence of cuttings and embankments keeps the line more or less level, then it drops down into a valley with the huge smooth swell of Waterpit Down rising on our right to shelter us from the relentless wind. The stream that owns this valley is in fact the River Camel, but we do not follow it far, turning off to the right on a short climb that brings us to Camelford station. This is another wide-open spot. Standing in the small goods yard is a lengthy rake of wagons, more are in the up platform with a goods brake van on the nearer end. The important daily goods train, the 9.30am from Yeoford which shunts every yard except poor little Egloskerry, has done its business and will follow us down after we have cleared the next section. Its engine is the usual 'N' class, parked on the 'slaughter house road', and her crew have strolled down to exchange greetings and news. Two parties alight to catch the Tintagel bus, and the guard blows his whistle.

Away from Camelford is a long right-hand curve which appears from the vantage point of the engine to go on and on until we must surely have turned back on our course towards Halwill, but it is immediately followed by an equally endless curve to the left. Here lies Milepost 241¾. *Chard* tips her nose down to start the descent to sea level at Wadebridge, 12 miles away; average gradient 1 in 90, ruling gradient 1 in 73. To keep speed around 50mph and give the passengers a smooth ride needs a delicate hand on the brake and intimate knowledge of the twists and turns of the road. A dozen shovelfuls of coal every few minutes will keep pressure around 200lb. But already the driver is pulling the brake handle down to steady her round the next bend, and anyone who suffers unduly from vertigo would be advised to move over to the right-hand side of the train before we reach Delabole.

Delabole slate quarry, which is claimed to be the biggest man-made excavation in Europe, may not figure largely in the tourist itinerary, but it is so important to the district that there was no question that the railway should come by it. Likewise, the quarry company regarded a rail-link as so important that when the railway

builders at last approached their property in the autumn of 1893 they provided land for three quarters of a mile of route without charge. Cornish fishermen, miners and farmers live their lives beneath slate roofs and thereafter rest beneath slate gravestones. The quarry itself is one of those few sights which are actually more spectacular than one anticipates. There is no advance indication of its presence; the train emerges from an ordinary little overbridge and we are looking straight down into the most gigantic hole. Moments later it is out of sight again and we are drawing into the station, a standard North Cornwall station with extra sidings curving round towards the quarry buildings. We have to wait a couple of minutes here for time before continuing down the helter-skelter, overlooking the village of St Teath which is not provided with a station. The two stopping points on the way down, Port Isaac Road and St Kew Highway, are sited as much for the purpose of dividing the line into sections as for the convenience of the populace, although they do adjoin main roads. The approach to Port Isaac Road is round a bend which really comes close to turning us around, from heading due west to heading southeast. On leaving it we pass through the only tunnel on the line, a curved bore below Trelil village, just 333yd long. One might expect more tunnels in Cornwall, since it is said that wherever there is a hole in the ground you will find a Cornishman at the bottom of it, but they have certainly done us proud in the matter of earthworks. For those who have lost count, there are 43 cuttings between Wadebridge and Launceston. The device handed over by the St Kew Highway signalman differs from the familiar single-line tablet. It is a key token; a development which is designed, as its name implies, to unlock lever frames. When it is operated in the lock it allows levers to be pulled and it is then retained in the lock until the levers are restored. Since you cannot proceed on your way without the token and you cannot retrieve the token from the frame without returning all points to normal, there is no chance of the next man coming along and finding points set the wrong way. Also at St Kew Highway we cross with the afternoon up goods. Hauled by the inevitable 2-6-0, it left Wadebridge at 4.40pm and some of its wagons loaded with slate, meat (dead or alive) or fish will be rumbling into Exmouth Junction at about midnight.

We leave St Kew Highway at 5pm, still heading downhill into a wooded ravine beside the little River Allen. The driver lets her run for

Above:
Cornish scenery is more open than that of Devon. The angle of the sun on this train running downhill near Trequite suggests that it may be the 5.51pm Okehampton-Padstow. No 34004 *Yeovil* (rebuilt in 1958) with a four-wheel van and two Maunsell BSKs in carmine and cream livery. B. A. Butt

Below:
On 16 May 1962, *66 Squadron* on the last leg beside the River Camel, with Wadebridge in the background. This engine, like *Chard*, never had an enamelled crest on the side.
S. C. Nash

Right:
On Midsummer Day 1962, the Wadebridge trio line up in front of their coal stage. The disposal road with ashpit lies behind 30586 in the middle; the shed is in the left background. The River Camel runs behind a bank to the bridge in the distance. *R. C. Riley*

about 3min, then shuts the regulator and puts in a little brake to hold her on the last descent, close by the stream now. He slows here a bit more, looking across to the fireman who is in his seat looking out for the Wadebridge outer home signals. Under a bridge and the valley opens out to our right. Two substantial girder bridges are in front, the Allen and, much wider, the River Camel. The fireman raises his hand and nods, the driver gives her just a little steam as she crosses the bridge with a creaking sound as the rear Bissell truck under our feet swings across on the sharp curve, and a sudden squeak from a tender-wheel flange. The line coming in on our left is the original Bodmin & Wadebridge main line. There is no physical junction just here, the two tracks continue side by side past what used to be Wadebridge Junction. Some 600yd ahead a very handsome four-arm bracket signal stands with the third arm from the left raised to beckon us in to Wadebridge station.

Many steam enthusiasts come to Wadebridge with no interest beyond the railway, and for them its most famous inhabitants are the three 'Beattie tanks'. One of them is shunting the goods yard when we arrive, having completed its main task of the day, a run up the original Bodmin and Wadebridge line to collect clay from Wenford Bridge. This little engine is a direct link with the first trains from Waterloo to Exeter. If we take away the top part of its cab and some modern appendages such as injectors and vacuum brake equipment, and give it a slightly smaller boiler with a feedwater heater standing up behind the chimney, we have the likeness of the locomotives designed by Joseph Beattie for the LSWR a century ago. The 2-4-0WTs now numbered 30585-7 are survivors of a type built during the 1870s for the London suburban workings. All the rest disappeared before the turn of the century, but these three were kept, repeatedly refurbished and modernised, on the grounds that they

were the only locomotives suitable for the Wenford Bridge trains, so here they are in the Space Age. Like the Celts of old, they have been driven westward by the tide of progress, now to be appreciated only by a few visitors who like to feel that here, at least, not everything is constantly being changed for change's sake. To the locals, waiting while these antiques are hand-flagged across the A389 at Dunmere Bridge, they are just a superannuated nuisance.

Wadebridge engine shed, a two-road building, situated between the station and the riverside meadow, has six residents; the Beattie tanks and three passenger tank engines, which were, until recently, of the LSWR '02' class, now being replaced by GWR pannier tanks. Nos 4666 and 4694 are on the strength with one remaining '02' No 30200. Several larger engines are also stabled overnight in readiness for the morning up workings, including at least two 'N' class and *Chard* herself.

Remote outpost though it may be, Wadebridge is at this moment giving a fair imitation of Clapham Junction in its way, for as soon as the 'ACE' is in, the road is reset to allow the 4.25pm from Bodmin General, drawn by a GWR 2-6-2T, to cross over into the loop platform. Meanwhile the 5.2pm Padstow-Bodmin North is, we hope, coming up from the west. There is a surge of activity, a couple of bicycles and a pram to be unloaded, someone asking our guard which is the Bodmin train, an altercation outside as a tractor and trailer is blocking the station entrance while trying to back up to the inconveniently adjacent goods shed. The driver is writing up his ticket and exchanging notes with a Wadebridge driver who will take over the engine later; the fireman puts some more water in his boiler before stepping over to look at the bookstall. At this point the up train rattles in: old No 30200, hauling two coaches and two vans. There is a

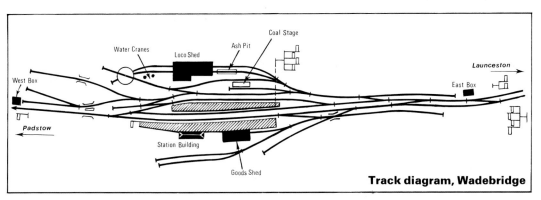

Track diagram, Wadebridge

Right:
The 'ACE' at Little Petherick Creek on 17 May 1962. On that day the engine was *Chard* herself. *S. C. Nash*

Below right:
On 13 May 1961, the ACE on the last few yards into Padstow, behind *92 Squadron* again. In view are Little Petherick Creek Bridge and Dennis Hill with its obelisk. *S. C. Nash*

Bottom right:
The end of the road. *Exmouth* and a BR Standard coach, overlooked by the Hotel Metropole, on 4 September 1964. *S. C. Nash*

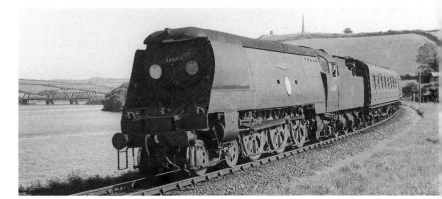

pause while everybody who should be on the 'ACE' gets back aboard, the Wadebridge West signalman reverses his points, opens the gates and pulls off both down signals, and at about 5.13pm we are off on the last lap.

Nine minutes is all that it takes, yet the traveller from London remembers this bit above all as pure Cornish enchantment. We slow briefly to pick up the tablet, pass the original Bodmin & Wadebridge sheds and quay, and emerge from the town alongside the broadening Camel estuary. Grey river mud gives way to golden sea sand, seen to best advantage at this time of day with autumn sunlight painting up the fields and farmhouses on the far bank. The fireman checks his fire,

trickles a few in across the back and takes his seat to watch the road and the scenery. A man painting a boat at Oldtown Cove turns and waves as the train passes on the causeway behind him. Speed is reduced to 15mph for Little Petherick Creek bridge, which consists of three 150ft trusses set on a curve, the train passes through a last rock cutting and we coast into Padstow station. Another standard North Cornwall station, nestling between the fish market and the Metropole Hotel, Padstow is 259¾ miles from Waterloo and a world apart from it. The 'ACE' comes to rest at 5.22pm.

The journey of the 'ACE' is now over, but *Chard* and her crew still have several tasks to perform. The first is to shunt the stock to clear

Above right:
The 6pm Padstow-Okehampton, which the Exmouth Junction crew work back from Wadebridge, is seen passing Padstow outer home and advance starter on 17 May 1962; 'N' class 2-6-0 No 31835 in charge.
S. C. Nash

Right:
66 Squadron works the 6.13pm Wadebridge-Padstow on 16 May 1962.
S. C. Nash

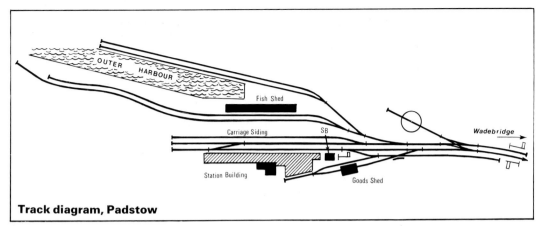

Track diagram, Padstow

the single platform for the 6pm train to Okehampton, which is parked on what used to be the dock siding. We uncouple the engine and ease her forward to the very end of the track, seemingly posing for a farewell to the passengers hurrying up Station Road. She then runs back, having to go quite a distance beyond the station on the run-round loop to regain the main line and come on to the other end of the train, pull it out and propel it into the carriage siding. While the train is doing this it is effectively occupying the Wadebridge-Padstow section, although it does not interfere with movements at the Wadebridge end because it is also under the protection of an advance starter at Padstow, so nothing can come down until it is safely 'inside'. The discipline of the block system reigns supreme. No other movement is possible, in fact, until *Chard* has returned tender-first to Wadebridge in order to work the 6.13pm to Padstow. During these manoeuvres her fire has been gradually burning away until the dead section at the back has burnt through. Thanks to the fireman's judgement, it does not reach this stage until we are on the way back to Wadebridge, so we do not disturb the old-world charm of the village by blowing-off. During the run he cracks the blower, runs the rake through the fire to ensure that no unburnt coal is congealing in it, and adds enough coal to keep it about a foot thick. There will be little demand for steam for the next hour; if his judgement proves inaccurate a few shovelfuls on the thin bright fire will catch quickly, while judicious use of the injector will keep pressure at around 220lb.

Chard arrives at Wadebridge at 5.44pm. The crew who have worked from Exeter get off here, in order to have their meal-break before working home on the 6pm Padstow-Okehampton, and a Wadebridge crew attach the locomotive to the single coach which forms the 6.13pm Wadebridge-Padstow and 6.27pm return. The use of a locomotive capable of handling the whole 'ACE' to haul a trailing load of 36 tons on a level route looks, one must admit, ridiculous; something the size of the Beattie tank could do the job. But the engine is there, the coach is there, and no one has yet produced a locomotive able to haul all types of traffic which is not too big most of the time. The only comfort is that *Chard*, when she is under-utilised, represents less capital lying idle than would an equivalent diesel-electric locomotive.

After bringing her coach back from Padstow, *Chard* arrives on Wadebridge shed at about 7pm. The driver pulls her up near the turntable and goes to report the arrival of the engine, information which is required back at Exmouth Junction so that her record may be made up to date with the mileage, while the fireman fills the tender tank. She is still facing 'down', but the turntable here is too short for her so she will be turned on the 65ft turntable at Padstow in the morning. She is then moved to stand by the small coal stage, and secured — hand-brake on, regulator shut, vacuum ejector off, cylinder cocks open, reverser to mid-gear. The driver goes round examining her for defects, withdrawing oil trimmings and checking oil levels in the lubricators. The fireman turns the blower on slightly and takes his shovel and brush forward to clear out the smokebox. Removal of the headboard (if it was not taken off before working the 6.13pm) reveals the two central door locking handles. The outer one unscrews, the inner one turns to disengage, and the fireman takes care not to fall off the front of the engine as the heavy door opens to reveal a smooth bed of fine cinders about 8in deep. Shovelling it out is an unpleasant job; it is impossible to clear the long smokebox without reaching well into it, and stirring the

Above:
Chard finishes her day on 17 May 1962 by returning the single coach to Wadebridge. On the far side of the estuary are Rock sand dunes and Porthilly Cove. *S. C. Nash*

'char' releases hot sulphurous fumes which the blower only partially pushes up the chimney. He brushes down the door before closing it. Back at the cab, the fire has now died down to a dull red. He opens the ashpan hoppers (a few old Devonshire epithets are used here, as it entails squeezing down beside the stage) and on the footplate releases the catches on the grate rocker levers. He pushes the live fire from the left half of the gate over to the right, adding a couple of shovelfuls of coal to keep it going, and rocks the left side grate to break up any clinker on it. This he pushes to the centre section which opens to drop it straight into the

pit. The process is repeated for the right-hand half of the grate, then the remaining fire is pulled into a heap under the door and banked up with coal. Down to the ground again to clear any ash which the outer hoppers have deposited on the rails, the fireman checks that the rear of the ashpan, where it is only 6in deep, is clear and shuts the hoppers. The driver has completed his examination and the depot coalman has replenished the tender, so she may be moved to stand at the east end of the shed.

Both injectors are started up to fill the boiler. While they are on, the cab floor is hosed down, tender hatch shut and cab gauges and handles wiped over. With no source of heat, feedwater entering the boiler knocks the pressure back fast and by the time the water is an inch from the top nut it is down to 100lb. A final clang as the injectors are shut down, and this vital, fiery giant of a machine is quiet and still, awaiting another day's work.

Right:
When disposing a Bulleid Pacific the ash from the side hoppers must be cleared off the rails. (the author at Bold Colliery in 1980). *E. W. J. Crawforth*

Valedictory

On the railway that we remember the trains always ran smoothly through a sunlit countryside, but in fact it was not always plain steaming, and in the autumn of 1960 storm clouds of more than one kind were gathering. At the end of September the south coast was hit by repeated deluges of rain, causing rivers to rise from their beds and take over the city streets and railway lines. At 8am on 30 September the River Taw, carrying the run-off from north Dartmoor, overwhelmed its bridge near North Tawton and washed over the track, while the River Yeo did the same near Crediton. The section between Crediton and Newton St Cyres, lying close to the river, was soon submerged and bridge No 547 disintegrated. Worse followed, for in the darkness of the next morning the newspaper train from Waterloo came to an abrupt halt on Honiton bank with its engine embedded in mud which had sloughed off the cutting-side. There were 30 separate slips and wash-outs on Honiton bank alone. Railwaymen, many of whose own homes were flooded, immediately set to work and reconnected the severed routes in a fortnight — a fine demonstration of the resilience of the system and the dedication of its staff.

The other storm was political and did not break for another couple of years. The new equipment being bought under the Modernisation Plan was impressive, but very expensive; with a dawning of understanding of what the bill would be to re-equip the whole railway system, there came a rising doubt that the public purse would stand it. A cold light was focused on the country stations and branch lines whose takings could never justify the use of technology intended for the most intensive trunk line traffic. When the Treasury finally panicked and demanded of the Railway Executive, 'What will we get for our money?' the reply was 'Let us operate like a commercial company and we will promise a financial return on your investment'. The upshot of that was the Transport Act of 1962, which abolished the British Transport Commission and established a British Railways Board (BRB), which differed from its predecessor in that it was no longer a common carrier. This meant that it could choose its trade like any other haulier with his lorry, so it promptly set about redrawing the railway map, grading every line and station according to the monetary value of its traffic. The plan was basically simple — having listed the services in order of profitability one could draw a line at a level which, when everything below it was discarded, would give a rate of return that would keep the British Taxpayer happy. When, in due course, the line was drawn, the entire Southern Region west of Salisbury lay below it.

This plan was opposed by those who valued railways (and who perceived the greater potential value of railways if they were used properly), but they were outgunned by big business, outnumbered by the freedom-of-the-open-road brigade and outmanoeuvred by politicians upon whose motives we can only speculate. The historical division between Southern and Western Region was replaced by geographical boundaries, putting everything west of Salisbury in the Western Region, which could see no point at all in having two main routes from London to Exeter and Plymouth. Therefore, at the close of the 1964 summer timetable the 'ACE' and all its ilk came to a summary end. All that tiresome coupling and uncoupling of through carriages ceased: the diesel railcars which now worked the branches

109

Above:
The last true multi-portion 'ACE' ran on Friday 4 September 1964. The Padstow part, including set No 565, was hauled by No 34015 *Exmouth*, and S. C. Nash was there to see it arrive. Holiday traffic was still busy, with at least twelve coaches stabled in the sidings between station and fish market.

could not in any case have hauled them. On the main line the smaller stations were closed, passenger trains became 'semi-fast' and terminated at Exeter St Davids. By 1968 goods traffic had virtually ceased and much of the Salisbury-Exeter route was reduced to single track.

The pollarding of the trunk line left the 'Withered Arm' out, as it were, on a limb, so although it remained largely intact for another two years its decline was inevitable. New railway policy precluded entertaining any kind of seasonal traffic (such as holidaymakers) on the grounds of unprofitability, while regular customers, faced with the prospect of losing the service, had to make other arrangements if they wanted to stay in business. As the West Country resounded to the roar of an ever-growing tide of motor traffic, a fraction of which would have made the railways rich beyond their fondest dreams, local councils paid lip service to the desirability of maintaining rail links and voted vast sums of money for road building.

So the closures began: Andover to Romsey in September 1964, the NDCJR in March 1965, Lyme Regis in November 1965, Seaton in March 1966, Chard, Yeovil and Bude in October 1966, Padstow in January 1967, Sidmouth in March 1967, Plymouth in May 1968, Ilfracombe in October 1970. On the main line Sutton Bingham station was abandoned at the end of 1962, followed by Hurstbourne in 1964 and several stations in March 1966. As 37 of the original 49 stations between Waterloo and Exeter were still open to passengers, the route was considered to have got off pretty lightly. Part of the NDCJR continued until October 1982, serving a clay quarry at Meeth, and the Wenford Bridge line — Cornwall's first railway

— was finally demolished in September 1985, in its 150th year. Another station which continued to host excursions was Okehampton, by virtue of the rail connection to Meldon Quarry, which still flourishes as the railway's source of ballast.

Then an amazing thing happened. The public continued to demand a train service and, more importantly, to use it, and the dismal downward spiral was reversed. The old negative management style was replaced by a positive approach. Some stations whose platforms had escaped destruction were reinstated as stopping places: Sidmouth Junction in 1971, Templecombe and Pinhoe in 1983. The singled main line began to prove, surprisingly enough, to be inadequate, so by the mid-1980s serious attempts began to replace more of the double track. For the branches and the routes west of Coleford Junction, however, it was already too late. The BRB was satisfied that North Cornwall would never again need a railway; bridges were flattened, embankments bulldozed and cuttings filled in; Seaton, Lyme and the rest seem content without railways, and even if they were not, the fact is that while it is quite easy to abandon a railway line it is a horrendously long and expensive affair to put it back again. The much-publicised cost of £435,000 to install a passing loop near Tisbury on the main line in 1985 speaks for itself.

What remains to see of the 'ACE', 30 years on? One can still travel from Waterloo to Exeter on a train service which is as good now as it has ever been. The 1988 timetable showed an hourly-interval service to Salisbury, with alternate trains continuing to Exeter; they all stop at most of the surviving stations and the best time of 3hr 1min compares well with those of past years. However, the goods sheds are either grassy mounds or have been sold off to other users who bring no business to the railway. Chard Junction, for example, is as busy as ever with milk, coal and timber, but all of it is transported by road lorries.

The rest of the route is just fragments. British Railways runs passenger trains from Exeter to Barnstaple Junction and from Plymouth to Gunnislake, on the Callington branch. Bits of civil engineering may be seen here and there: Meldon viaduct still stands because it provides access to the quarry, Holsworthy viaduct, a pioneer concrete structure, is intact but derelict. In West Devon and Cornwall, where trackbeds have been sold off, many of the stations have passed into private ownership and are prized for their sturdy construction. Torrington and Barnstaple Town are restaurants, Bideford is a bank. Of the 12 standard North Cornwall stations, only Tower Hill and Launceston were demolished; there are private residences, a hotel at St Kew Highway,

and a camp site at Otterham. On the other hand, Okehampton waits for ghost trains, Halwill is a tragic sleeping beauty, and Wadebridge and Bude are housing estates (look for Bulleid Way at the latter). Padstow is a car park. The line from Wadebridge to Padstow has been adopted as a public footpath; the vistas of the Camel estuary, which only the lengthman was able to pause and savour in the old days, are as glorious as ever. Sir John Betjeman, the 'ACE's' own bard, did not forget his favourite coast and was laid to rest here; a community centre at Wadebridge which incorporates the remains of the station being dedicated to his memory.

On a brighter note, the Bodmin & Wadebridge Railway still exists, albeit in a much altered form. A new company was formed with the intention of reinstating first the Great Western branch from Bodmin Road to Bodmin General, the connection to Boscarne Junction, and later the original Wenford Bridge line which may see a scheduled passenger service for the first time in its history. A smaller but equally welcome development has taken place at Launceston. Although the site of the two stations has been redeveloped, a couple of miles of trackbed westwards up the Kensey valley was not violated and is now once more a railway. The Launceston Steam Railway has laid a 2ft gauge line with full supporting amenities. The result in no way represents anything that used to run in Cornwall, but it is a highly professional little railway which should be studied by all countryside authorities.

It is also still possible to ride in one of the incomparably comfortable Bulleid coaches behind a 'West Country', 2-6-0 or 'M7', although to do so one must leave 'ACE' territory and visit the Bluebell Railway in Sussex or Swanage on the Dorset coast, both railways which were discarded by the throw-

away generation and are being painstakingly rebuilt. Brake Second Corridor No 2515 or Second Open No 1464 are typical of the stock used for West Country services. It is sadly true, however, that although engines were preserved in abundance, coaches were not, and although Bulleid coaches exist in ones and twos in various places, the total is only around 20.

Representatives of all six generations of locomotives survive, although it should be borne in mind that the enormous cost to voluntary resources of maintaining them means that, for both locomotives and coaches, there are wide variations from year to year in regard to which examples are operating or even on display.

Two of the Beattie tanks were saved, No 30585 at the Buckinghamshire Railway Centre and No 30587 by the National Railway Museum (NRM) but currently on loan to the Dart Valley Railway. Of William Adams' graceful engines, 'T3' class 4-4-0 No 563 is in the NRM and 4-4-2T No 30583 has been a resident of the Bluebell Railway for longer than she spent working the Lyme Regis branch. The few remaining Drummond locomotives all had remarkable escapes, not least 'M7' No 30053, owing her existence to an American benefactor and now back at Swanage where she must stand for all the South Western branch trains. The sole surviving Drummond 4-4-0, 'Greyhound' No 120 was fortunate in being laid aside for the NRM and, after many years in a rusty limbo, restored to life again. A similar story followed the only Urie 'N15' 4-6-0 No 777 *Sir Lamiel*, which under the stewardship of the Humberside Locomotive Preservation Group returned during the 1980s to the haulage of main line express trains on special occasions, demonstrating how she used to haul the 'ACE' before World War 2. There are also several examples of the similar 'S15' running, including Exmouth Junction's No 841. The 'U' and 'N' class 2-6-0s are represented by Nos 1618 and 1638 on the Bluebell Railway and Nos 1625, 1806 and 1874 on the Mid-Hants Railway.

And what of the last generation of steam, the Bulleid 'Merchant Navies' and 'West Countries'? When SR steam operation ceased in 1967, few people believed that 20 years later a steam-hauled train would be seen doing a mile a minute on the LSWR main line. Yet it happened, and *Clan Line* was the engine.

Two organisations were set up to preserve Bulleid engines, the Bulleid Society and the Merchant Navy Locomotive Preservation Society. Despite the interest shown by enthusiasts in the last few years of Southern steam,

when it came to expressing enthusiasm in hard cash there was only enough to buy two engines: No 34023 *Blackmore Vale* and No 35028 *Clan Line*. The former, believing that the best future lay with the independent railways, found a home on the Bluebell. The latter joined the campaign to bring steam to British Railways, and years of steady, patient work brought their reward when *Clan Line* hauled an excursion from Basingstoke to Salisbury and Westbury on 27 April 1974. That proved to be the last steam train through Salisbury for 12½ years, but in 1986, following the improvement in the line's fortunes, the new custodians invited *Clan Line* back.

There were by then no facilities at all for servicing steam engines, with one exception, but the technique of off-base operation was now well-understood, and a converted coach parked in the down bay on Salisbury station served the functions of a Motive Power Depot. The one exception to the lack of facilities was the turntable at Yeovil Junction which has continued to be used by the permanent way engineers. Use of this and the reinstated triangle at Laverstock permitted steam-hauled trips between Salisbury and Yeovil Junction. The schedule of 75min for the 39 miles was not fast by 1960 standards, but our preserved locomotives do not have to prove anything in the matter of speed, and times have changed. But different times or no, in the writer's view there was one name above all others that should be carried on the front of the engine for her return to the SWR. It was about 3.0am on 29 September 1986 when *Clan Line* steamed into Salisbury station, complete with Plymouth headcode and 'ACE' board, and there wasn't a dry eye in the house.

There is more to the Bulleid story, for contrary to what was expected, after 1967 several engines remained in existence, and at the time of writing are being used as the bases for some ambitious reconstructions, some so extensive that it is the design which is being preserved rather than the machines. *Chard* is not among them, as she was broken up in 1966, but if all the rebuild projects succeed the total number of workable engines will rise to 10 'Merchant Navies' and 17 'West Countries'. Clearly, the wealth of skill, determination, occasional heroism and sheer solid graft which drove the 'ACE' on its course are alive and flourishing, and even though it may not appear again in the places, and in the guise, described in this account, we may be sure that, whatever sea-changes it undergoes, the name and spirit of this famous train will run on through our future.